CREATING YOUR OWN NETSCAPE WEB PAGES

Liz's Delivery Service
You say what, we say how!

P9-AOR-471

r materials
ethod below

ist of WWW Links

keeps their own list of "cool" links. This is my list of links that I actually use and reference.

Links
ice Hall Publishing
millan Publishing
Davis Net
On-Line
dwatch Magazine
le Magazine
s Links
SmartNotes Magazin
Notes Resources
e on the Web
ipware Links
abra Share
ing neat HTML featur
am (integrated movem
ime Audio
Audio Home Page
ware Development C

ist Elemen

en to set up
n, and Numl
s in Definitio
<dd> for the
he browser's
ing in the U

t ☒ What's New Too!
Web Worm ☒ Apollo

center ☐ NIKOS

http://

Category:
Health & Fitness ▼ If Other, please Specify

e - [Barney's Circus Page: Elephants]
ew Go Bookmarks Options Directory

Start | Micros... | Nets... | Netsco | Explori | HotDo... | Conne... | WinQV... | Telnet -

The Elephant Page in Barney's Circus

There are over 25 elephants that make up the mammoth creature ent
Barney's circus. We have elephants from all over the world, includin
extremely rare albino elephant. You won't want to miss any of these
creatures here at Barney's Circus.

- The Albino Elephant (63K)
- African Elephants (32K)
- More Elephant Pictures
- Watch the elephant performance (video - 3 meg)
- Buy an elephant ride today!

Other Ele

Unknown File Type

No Viewer Configured for File Type: application/octet

N How would you like to handle this file?

Save to Disk   Cancel Transfer   Configure a Vie

Tags

Netscape - [
File Edit View

Welcome to Andy's Home

All visitors are welcome!

Thanks for stopping by my web page. It is an ongoing project and will probably not be finished until Chapter 10 of this b
am getting ready to graduate from **The Ohio State University** and hope to pursue a full time job writing, creating we

ompact List
Multi-column

que ®

Internet

CREATING YOUR OWN NETSCAPE WEB PAGES

Andrew Bryce Shafran
Don Doherty

que®

Creating Your Own Netscape Web Pages

Copyright© 1995 by Que® Corporation

Library of Congress Catalog No.: 95-71415

ISBN: 0-7897-0621-0

97 96 95   6 5 4 3 2 1

Interpretation of the printing code: the rightmost double-digit number is the year of the book's printing; the rightmost single-digit number, the number of the book's printing. For example, a printing code of 95-1 shows that the first printing of the book occurred in 1995.

Screen reproductions in this book were created using Collage Plus from Inner Media, Inc., Hollis, NH.

Composed in *1 Stone Serif* and *MCPdigital* by Que Corporation

Credits

President
Roland Elgey

Publisher
Stacy Hiquet

Publishing Director
Brad R. Koch

Editorial Services Director
Elizabeth Keaffaber

Managing Editor
Sandy Doell

Director of Marketing
Lynn E. Zingraf

Senior Series Editor
Chris Nelson

Acquisitions Editor
Beverly M. Eppink

Product Director
Mark Cierzniak

Production Editor
Elizabeth A. Bruns

Assistant Product Marketing Manager
Kim Margolius

Technical Writers
Noel Estabrook
John Jung

Technical Editor
Marty Wyatt

Technical Specialist
Cari Skaggs

Acquisitions Coordinator
Ruth Slates

Operations Coordinator
Patty Brooks

Editorial Assistant
Andrea Duvall

Book Designer
Ruth Harvey

Cover Designer
Dan Armstrong

Production Team
Angela D. Bannan
Jason Carr
Aleata Howard
John Hulse
Daryl Kessler
Bobbi Satterfield
Michael Thomas
Scott Tullis
Karen York

Indexer
Kathy Venable

About the Author

Andrew Bryce Shafran is a full-time writer and computer consultant based out of Columbus, Ohio. He is a student at The Ohio State University, and is 100% Buckeye. Born in Columbus, Andy has worked extensively with Lotus Notes and the Lotus Smartsuite.

He loves writing books and magazine articles, especially about CompuServe and the WWW. His other Que books include *The Complete Idiot's Guide to CompuServe* and *Easy Lotus Notes for Windows*, just to name a few.

When he's not writing, he enjoys live theater, particularly Broadway shows, and you can often find him walking around Times Square in New York City.

Acknowledgments

First and foremost, I'd like to thank Elizabeth Muska for helping me in her many ways on this project and reminding me that it's enjoyable to see sunlight every now and then.

I'd also like to thank my editors at Que, Beverly Eppink and Brad Koch, for giving me the opportunity to write such an enjoyable and maniacally-scheduled book. Thanks again to them and Mark Cierzniak for working with my ludicrous editing schedule so that I could make my vacation flight in time.

We'd Like to Hear from You!

As part of our continuing effort to produce books of the highest possible quality, Que would like to hear your comments. To stay competitive, we *really* want you, as a computer book reader and user, to let us know what you like or dislike most about this book or other Que products.

You can mail comments, ideas, or suggestions for improving future editions to the address below, or send us a fax at (317) 581-4663. For the online inclined, Macmillan Computer Publishing has a forum on CompuServe (type **GO QUEBOOKS** at any prompt) through which our staff and authors are available for questions and comments. The address of our Internet site is **http://www.mcp.com** (World Wide Web).

In addition to exploring our forum, please feel free to contact me personally to discuss your opinions of this book: I'm #76245,476 on CompuServe, and I'm mcierzniak@que.mcp.com on the Internet.

Thanks in advance—your comments will help us to continue publishing the best books available on computer topics in today's market.

Mark Cierzniak
Product Development Specialist
Que Corporation
201 W. 103rd Street
Indianapolis, Indiana 46290
USA

Contents at a Glance

Contents

8 Advanced and Cool Ways to Customize Your Home Page   137

V Adding the Final Touches to Your Web Page   155

9 Forms, Clickable Images, and Beyond   157

Appendix A   Affordable Web Providers   205

Appendix B   References Used In This Book   213

Appendix C   Home Page Final Check List   217

Appendix D   What's on the CD-ROM?   219

Introduction

Welcome to *Creating Your Own Netscape Web Pages*. This book will guide you through the entire process of setting up your own personal Web page from start to finish.

In this Introduction, I'll talk about important information you'll want to remember while reading this book. I'll describe who this book is for, what kind of information you can find inside, what assumptions I've made, and why this is the best—and only—book you'll need for getting on the World Wide Web.

So read on and enjoy learning how to create your own home page.

What You'll Learn In This Book

This book is geared toward teaching you what you need to know about home page publishing. I'll take you step by step through the entire process, from concept to finished product.

Specifically, you'll learn how to:

- Plan your home page

- Effectively use an HTML editor

- Make your home page available immediately

- Organize information with lists and tables

- Link your home page to others throughout the world

- Incorporate other Internet resources, such as FTP and Gopher, into your home page

- Embed pictures, audio clips, and video clips into your home page

- Use proper home page design techniques

- Maintain your home page to keep it current and interesting

- Attract visitors from around the world to your home page

Practical Explanations, not Concepts

I'm going to take you through the real life issues that you face while creating your home page. You'll have to decide what kind of information to put on your home page, how to organize it, which links you should include, and how to keep your page up-to-date in the future.

I'm not going to waste much of your time writing about the intricacies of HTML, arguments over Internet bandwidth, or other issues that probably don't interest you. Instead, you'll find a step by step guide to help you accomplish all your home page goals.

Introduction to HTML Tools, not HTML Tutorial

Home pages are written in Hyper Text Markup Language (HTML). While HTML is not overly difficult, some concepts can be hard to understand and work with.

That's why I've chosen to include a special HTML editor with this book. Using this editor, you won't have to learn all the details of HTML Programming. Instead you can use the HTML editor to take care of the programming for you. You don't need to be an HTML expert to have a great-looking home page.

Who Is This Book for?

Anyone who has experienced the World Wide Web, and wants to create his or her own unique home page, will be interested in this book. In general, the beginner and average level World Wide Web surfer and Internet user will find this book a suitable and complete tool for creating home pages.

I have made a couple of assumptions about you, the reader, while writing this book:

You've seen the Web—It's important that you understand what the World Wide Web is, and have a rudimentary understanding of how it works (I'll go over this in more detail in the first chapter). You should know the difference between Netscape (a WWW Browser) and Microsoft Excel (not a browser). You don't have to be an Internet guru, but passing familiarity helps.

You have an Internet SLIP/PPP Connection—This book doesn't cover how to get up and running with an Internet connection that lets you access the World Wide Web. It does, however, talk about special places on the Internet to put your home page if you don't know where to place it. A general Internet reference book (such as *Using the Internet,* also published by Que) will help you get running and using the Web very quickly.

How This Book Helps You Create Your Home Page

Creating Your Own Netscape Web Pages is organized in order of difficulty of the tasks I present. The book starts with planning your home page and continues through the development cycle until your initial page is complete and you announce your home page to the Web world.

Each chapter is broken down into edible chunks of information that make it easy to digest the process of creating a home page. Think of each chapter as a new lesson in the learning process.

Here is a brief summary of what you'll find in this book and how it is organized:

Part I: Planning Your Web Page

This part includes the first two chapters of the book. Chapter 1 gives a basic introduction to the World Wide Web and contains important information detailing how the Web works. You'll also learn what a home page is.

In chapter 2, I discuss how to go about planning and organizing your home page as well as show you several different example home pages that already exist on the WWW. You'll be introduced to Hotdog, the HTML editor used throughout the book, and learn what to look for in a Web Provider (a vendor who stores your home page on the Internet for a monthly charge).

Part II: Creating a Basic Web Page

Read through this part to get up to speed on the basics of creating a home page. Chapter 3 overviews how to add text and text formatting features to your home page while keeping the information easy to read. In addition, you'll also learn how to break up blocks of text and what elements of HTML every Web page should have.

Continue on with chapter 4 for an explanation of how to use and include tables and lists into your home page. This chapter not only explains how to use lists and tables effectively, but also helps you decide when you want to use them as well.

Part III: Spicing Up Your Web Page

Part III helps you add some personality to your home page. Text and tables are nice looking, but most attractive home pages include images and links to other sites on the WWW. Chapter 5 teaches you how to integrate graphics and pictures into your home page. You'll learn how to use some of the images from the included CD-ROM or pictures of your own as important parts of your page.

In chapter 6, I show you how to add and organize hypertext links to your home page. You'll learn how to link your document to any other spot on the Web. In addition, you'll see how to use graphics as hotlinks and how to sort and organize links without overwhelming people browsing your page.

Part IV: Advanced Home Page Publishing

This part shows you how to use some of the cool advanced features of the Web, right in your own home page. Chapter 7 shows you that images are just the beginning to a multimedia home page. You'll learn how to add sound bites and video clips to your home page for a dazzling effect.

Continue on to chapter 8 where I'll demonstrate advanced ways to customize your home page. You'll learn how to incorporate additional World Wide Web and Netscape features by splitting your home page into several different pages, tracking the number of visitors who stop by and browse, and using other Internet resources (such as FTP and UseNet) as part of your home page.

Part V: Adding the Final Touches to Your Home Page

Before your home page is completed, you should read through Part V and learn how to clean up and publicize your home page on the Internet. In chapter 9, I'll run through examples on how to create clickable images for your home page. You'll find that clickable images will give your page a dynamic edge. Read chapter 10 to learn several important design considerations regarding home page publishing. You'll learn design issues that will make your page(s) exciting to look at and easy to maintain in the future.

In the final chapter of the book, chapter 11, I'll teach you how to let other WWW users know that your home page exists—what good is a home page that no one ever visits? You'll learn the proper channels of publicity, and where to announce to the Internet that you're ready for them to stop by and see the fruits of your labor, and I'll discuss some future developments on the horizon.

Appendixes

Several appendixes are provided for your benefit. Use them as references for the book and while you are creating your home page.

Appendix A: Web Page Providers—Your current Internet provider may not allow you to have your own personal home page, or they might charge you an arm and a leg. Here is a list of Web Page Providers that are extremely affordable and will cater to your specific needs.

Appendix B: WWW References—This book contains several references to many different sites on the World Wide Web. This appendix lists all referenced URLs and additional sites on the Web to help you create cool home pages.

Appendix C: Home Page Final Checklist—This appendix contains a simple checklist to make sure you've caught most of the common mistakes new home page creators make. I've summarized some of the common tips and tricks.

Appendix D: What's on the CD-ROM?—This appendix lists the files and an explanation of what is included on the CD-ROM found in the back of this book.

What's on the CD-ROM?

On the included CD-ROM in the back of the book, you'll find hundreds of megs of useful files that will assist you in creating your home page. You'll find everything from an easy to use sample home page template to professional caliber graphics and image editors.

You'll also find an impressive array of graphics, icons, and multimedia clips that you are free to use at will in your home page. Also included on the CD-ROM are several tools that will make Web Publishing easier. Hotdog and several other HTML editors, and additional WWW Viewer programs are also included.

Specifically, you'll find:

- Hotdog, the HTML Editor used in this book
- Media viewers for use with Netscape
- Graphics, pictures, and icons that are royalty-free for use in your home page
- Audio and video clips to add a new dimension to your page

- HTML validation tools

- Additional HTML creation and maintenance tools.

Programs Used In This Book

This book is meant to be used as a tutorial, taking you through the process of using your computer to create your own home page. There are several computer programs that can help in this process, and in this book I highlight two of them: Netscape, and Hotdog. Combined with this book, Netscape and Hotdog will guide you through any of the rough waters in the home page creation process.

Netscape

Netscape is the world's leading WWW Browser. It is estimated that up to 80% of all WWW traffic comes from Internet surfers who use Netscape. Netscape's popularity is no fluke, the browser has many attractive features that make it number one, including its price—free.

In addition, Netscape uses Web technology to the fullest extent. Several advanced textual and graphical formatting HTML features are only supported by Netscape (these features are termed Netscape extensions), as well as more efficient and faster access when connecting to different WWW sites.

I'll describe in chapter 2 where you can find and install the latest version of Netscape.

Hotdog

Hotdog is a top-notch HTML editor that takes the bite out of HTML programming and publishing. Using Hotdog, you don't have to be familiar with all the intricacies of HTML codes, tags, and special characters. Instead, Hotdog takes care of many of these complications.

Created in Australia, Hotdog, in my personal opinion, is the best of the available HTML editors. A shareware version is included on the CD-ROM in the back of this book, and I'll show you how install it in chapter 2. The rest of the book focuses on using Hotdog to create your Web Page and simplifying the process.

Conventions Used In this Book

As you're reading through the book, I use several different conventions that highlight specific types of information that you'll want to take note of.

All HTML codes and tags will appear in FULL CAPS. That's so you can tell the difference between text that appears on-screen, and text that tells Netscape what to do. Netscape doesn't care whether your HTML tags are in full caps. In addition, all URLs that I mention will be displayed in **boldface**. You can type them directly into your Netscape and go directly to the site I am referring to.

While working with the HTML editor provided, any text you type, as well as the HTML editor and browser buttons and commands you select, appear in **boldface**.

Besides these standard textual conventions, I use several different icons throughout this book.

Netscape Only

This icon means that the specific HTML tag or feature you are using only displays correctly when using Netscape as your WWW browser. Other browsers will likely ignore these tags.

On the CD-ROM

You can find referenced files, graphics, and templates on the CD-ROM found in the back of this book. This icon tells you where you can find the associated files on the CD-ROM.

Tip

Additional information that offers extra advice for creating your own Web Page are found as tips. I included personal anecdotal experiences, as well as specific design techniques in these extra bullets of information.

Caution

Actions that could make permanent changes or potentially cause problems in the future are highlighted as cautions. You'll want to take note of the caution sections because they could warn of an irreversible decision, or prevent damage your home page.

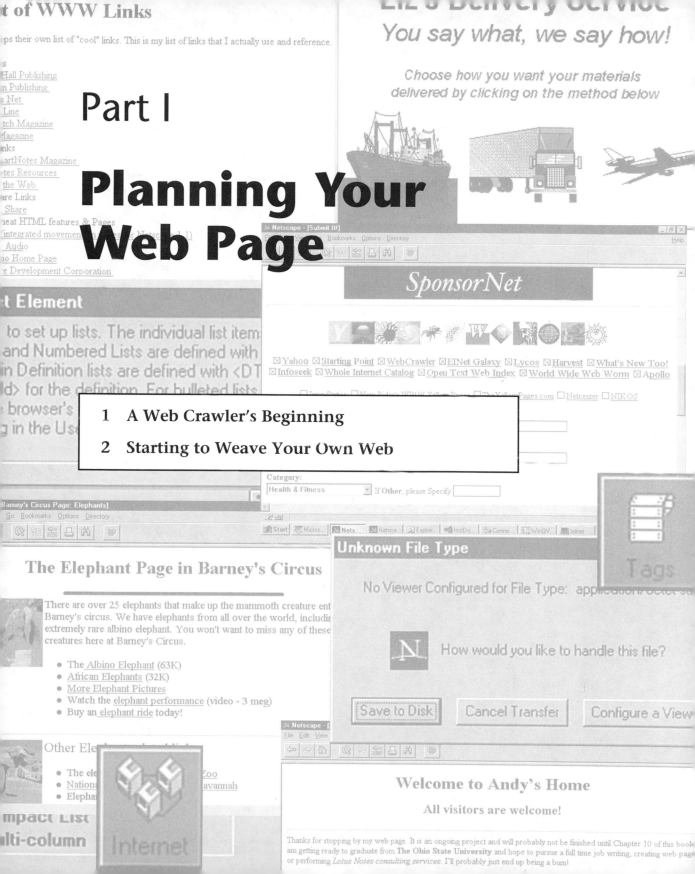

Part I

Planning Your Web Page

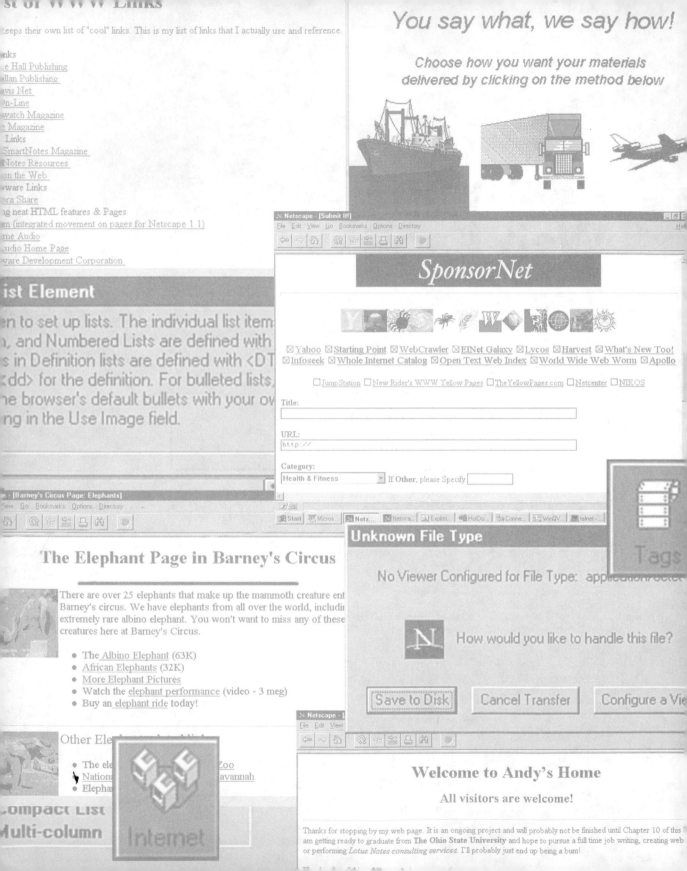

of WWW Links

keeps their own list of "cool" links. This is my list of links that I actually use and reference.

nks
e Hall Publishing
llan Publishing
vis Net
n-Line
watch Magazine
e Magazine
Links
SmartNotes Magazine
Notes Resources
on the Web
ware Links
ra Share
g neat HTML features & Pages
m (integrated movement on pages for Netscape 1.1)
me Audio
udio Home Page
ware Development Corporation

ist Element

en to set up lists. The individual list item
, and Numbered Lists are defined with
s in Definition lists are defined with <DT
<dd> for the definition. For bulleted lists,
e browser's default bullets with your ow
ng in the Use Image field.

You say what, we say how!

Choose how you want your materials
delivered by clicking on the method below

N Netscape - [Submit It!]
File Edit View Go Bookmarks Options Directory — Hel

SponsorNet

☒ Yahoo ☒ Starting Point ☒ WebCrawler ☒ EINet Galaxy ☒ Lycos ☒ Harvest ☒ What's New Too!
☒ Infoseek ☒ Whole Internet Catalog ☒ Open Text Web Index ☒ World Wide Web Worm ☒ Apollo

☐ JumpStation ☐ New Rider's WWW Yellow Pages ☐ TheYellowPages.com ☐ Netcenter ☐ NIKOS

Title:

URL:
http://

Category:
Health & Fitness ▾   If Other, please Specify

Start | Micros... | Nets... | Netsca... | Explor... | HotDo... | Conne... | WinQV | telnet -

Unknown File Type

No Viewer Configured for File Type: application/octe

How would you like to handle this file?

Save to Disk   Cancel Transfer   Configure a Vie

Tags

— [Barney's Circus Page: Elephants]
iew Go Bookmarks Options Directory

The Elephant Page in Barney's Circus

There are over 25 elephants that make up the mammoth creature en
Barney's circus. We have elephants from all over the world, includir
extremely rare albino elephant. You won't want to miss any of these
creatures here at Barney's Circus.

- The Albino Elephant (63K)
- African Elephants (32K)
- More Elephant Pictures
- Watch the elephant performance (video - 3 meg)
- Buy an elephant ride today!

Other Ele

- The ele Zoo
- Nationa avannah
- Elepha

N Netscape -
File Edit View

Welcome to Andy's Home

All visitors are welcome!

Thanks for stopping by my web page. It is an ongoing project and will probably not be finished until Chapter 10 of this
am getting ready to graduate from **The Ohio State University** and hope to pursue a full time job writing, creating web
or performing *Lotus Notes consulting services*. I'll probably just end up being a bum!

ompact List
ulti-column

Internet

Chapter 1

A Web Crawler's Beginning

By the time you've picked up this book and decided to create your own home page, you will have spent several hours "surfing" the Internet and exploring the World Wide Web. In this chapter, I introduce and explain the Web, and make sure you understand several concepts before creating your own home page.

A new chain of stores is popping up around the nation. These stores carry video and sound equipment, a fully stocked inventory of albums, CDs, and software, as well as a complete bookstore. They are true "multimedia" stores—more like warehouses, actually. Now, let's take that same concept and make it available electronically. What do you have?—the World Wide Web. But there's much more to know about the Web than this. In this chapter, you'll learn about:

- What the World Wide Web is

- How the Web works

- The history and future of the Web

- HTML (HyperText Markup Language)

- What a Home Page is

What Is the World Wide Web?

Simply put, the World Wide Web is a graphical way of retrieving information from the Internet. Using the Web, you can find information relating to any topic imaginable, right from your home computer. With a graphical and fun interface, you can browse through pages and pages of text, scan through tons of pictures, and even experience some audio and video clips. The WWW even integrates with other popular parts of the Internet such as Gopher and FTP, making it your one-stop shopping trip for exploring the Internet.

A textbook definition of the Web might be: "a multimedia, hypertext environment using a markup language that supports multiple Internet protocols." That's a good definition of the WWW if you completely understand what it means. Let me break down that sentence for you, just in case.

Multimedia

While most of the information found on the Internet is in straight text format, sometimes a picture is worth a thousand words (or more). One of the main features of the WWW is the ability to view images and text alike on the same screen. That makes using the Web graphical, fun and exciting (see fig.1.1).

Besides pictures and images, audio bites or video clips are also a cornerstone of the Web. Any site on the Web can integrate all four types of media into a single WWW page.

Movie studios regularly take advantage of the multimedia facets of the Web. On one screen you can read a movie review, see a picture of the movie poster, hear an actor recount his experience, and even see a preview of the movie at the same time.

Fig. 1.1
An example of multimedia in the movie "The Net" home page (**http:// www.spe.sony. com/Pictures/ SonyMovies/ netmulti.html**).

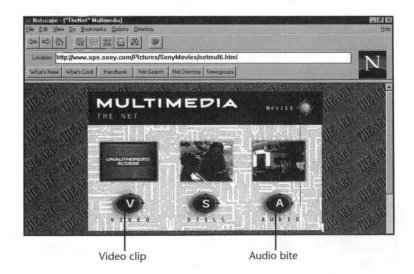

Video clip   Audio bite

Hypertext Links

The Web is what's called a "Hypertext" environment. Hypertext means that certain information that you see is "linked" to other pieces of information. For instance, when you use the Help feature in software such as Word or Excel, there are highlighted words that, by clicking on them, take you to help for that word. Similarly, by clicking your mouse on a Hypertext link, you automatically bring up the linked information as a separate document.

These Hypertext links are the basic building blocks of the Web. Every document is comprised of links that take you to other Web sites, pictures, sound, files and other related information.

On the WWW, these different places and links are called Universal Resource Locators (URLs). Every document and file on the Internet has its own unique URL that allows it be linked to other documents easily. You can think of these URLs as addresses. Each address has three basic elements:

- **URL Type**: The beginning of each URL identifies the type of link it is. For instance, http:// indicates a Web link, Gopher:// indicates a Gopher link, FTP:// indicates a link to an FTP site, and so on.

- **Domain**: Following the URL type is the actual Domain Name, or address, of the URL. For instance, Microsoft's Web address is www.microsoft.com, so their URL would be http://www.microsoft.com/

- **Directory or Document**: If a link is going to a particular document or directory, this would be attached to the end of the URL. For example, Microsoft has some shortcuts to the Internet in a document called ShortCuts.htm in the /Misc directory. So if you wanted to access this document, the entire URL would be http://www.microsoft.com/Misc/ShortCuts.htm

Let's say you were looking at a Web page of a circus, as in figure 1.2. Since this is a fictitious home page designed for this chapter, it does not have a URL. From this screen you can link to other pages that show you more information about each of the attractions, animals, and performers. The links to other places are usually underlined or appear in a different color so they're easy to identify.

Fig. 1.2

The circus home page is only the beginning of my quest for elephant knowledge.

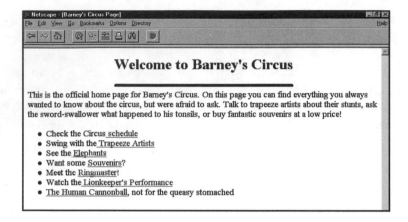

If you select the link to the elephants, you'll be brought to the circus elephant home page (see fig. 1.3). You can see a description of the elephant performances, and even a few neat pictures. There are also additional links that bring you to other elephant-related resources on the Web. These links have nothing to do with the circus, but are interesting to people who like elephants. You can follow links to zoos or African Savannahs, or maybe even learn about an elephant graveyard.

Fig. 1.3

This page links to all the elephant pages in the circus as well as other WWW pages.

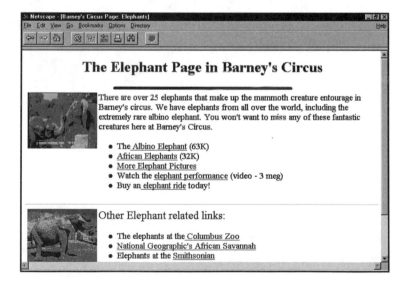

That's how the Web works. Related information is linked together in any way you choose. It's extremely flexible and friendly to use hypertext.

HTML

The World Wide Web is based on a programming language called **HyperText Markup Language** (HTML). HTML is a sub-set of an existing, more complicated language named SGML (but we won't go into that here).

A markup language uses tags that are inserted into textual documents that explain how information should be formatted on-screen. All HTML documents are purely text-based. Web browsers, such as Netscape, read the HTML documents and determine how to display that information on-screen. For example, the tag:

<b>This is <i>my</i> home page</b>

would bold the entire line as well as display "my" in italics.

Tags determine which text should appear larger (as headlines), how paragraphs are formatted, where graphics should be placed, and how to link to other WWW pages as in the example in figure 1.4. You'll learn all about the proper usage of tags as you read through this book.

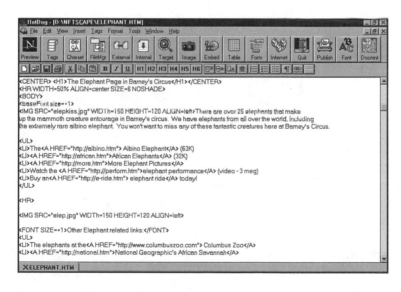

Fig. 1.4
Here's the same elephant home page in HTML format. Quite a difference!

Planning Web Pages

I

Internet Protocols

There's a lot more to the Web than simply hyperlinking thousands of different documents together. The Web uses its own communications device, the HTTP protocol, to send and receive pages back and forth across the Internet. HTTP (which stands for HyperText Transfer Protocol) is an Internet protocol that allows two computers to talk to each other in a specified format. However, HTTP is not the only Internet protocol supported by the WWW.

Using the Web and HTML, you can integrate the following Internet applications into your Web pages:

- **UseNet**—For access to Newsgroups around the world

- **FTP**—Used for uploading and downloading files using File Transfer Protocol

- **Gopher**—A menu-based "low-level" version of the Web which links different resources on the Internet

- **WAIS (Wide Area Information Service)**—Provides a way to search a variety of different databases.

- **Telnet**—Allows you to directly connect to other computers on the Internet

- **E-mail**—For sending messages across the world electronically.

The Web gives you convenient access to all of these different Internet services together in one place.

How the Web Works

This is the only section where I am going to go into more technical detail about the underlying way the World Wide Web works. As you explore the Web and start creating your own home page, you'll find it useful to understand the different pieces that comprise the Web and how they all fit together.

Client-Server Based

The Web is a "client-server" application. Client-server means that somewhere there exists a computer running Web server software and many different users (like you and me) are clients, using Web browsers, accessing information from the Web server.

Web servers help send information back and forth to users across the world, they maintain connections with other Web servers, and they keep track of important usage statistics, such as the number of visitors to a specific Web page. Currently, there are nearly 50,000 Web servers on the Internet that are constantly talking to each other.

Perhaps you can think of it this way. Each Web server contains all of the protocols and information available on a particular site. Where the documents are, whether there are executable programs which can be accessed, and more are all contained on the Web server. When you use Netscape to then access that Web site, the server jumps into action by providing the information that Netscape is requesting.

To use a previous example, when you tell Netscape to "go" to http://www.microsoft.com/Misc/ShortCuts.htm, Microsoft's Web server first interprets your request from Netscape, then finds the /Misc directory, locates the ShortCuts.htm document and "serves" the contents of that document to Netscape. Finally, Netscape takes that information, and translates the code in the file into a viewable document.

Note

Since the Web is a distributed system with servers across the globe, there is no central main Web server that controls the others. Thus, if a particular Web server becomes inactive, all of the other servers operate fine in its absence. If there was one central computer that ran into problems, 7 million Web surfers would be out of luck.

SLIP/PPP Connection Required

Access to the Web requires a special Internet connection that is client-server based. SLIP (Serial Line Internet Protocol) and PPP (Point-to-Point Protocol) connections allow Internet users to download useful information to their computers so they can retrieve it quicker the next time they need that information. SLIP and PPP connections also allow you to perform several tasks at one time. You can browse the Web, download e-mail, and read news all at once.

Without these connections, you can not use Netscape and many of the other cool resources on the Internet. The "opposite" of a SLIP or PPP connection is a simple shell account which will only allow you to use a textual interface to the Internet. Therefore, it's important to make sure that you request SLIP or PP access from your Internet Service Provider (ISP).

Once you have such a connection, you will also need software that will allow your computer to "talk" in these protocols. Many ISPs provide this software with their service. On a PC, a Winsock (Windows Socket) client such as Trumpet Winsock is often used.

> ## Caution
>
> Since you will be using your SLIP or PPP connection to transfer a lot of data (graphics, audio and other resources take up a lot of room), you will want to also make sure you have a high-speed modem. A 14.4 modem is sufficient, but using a 28.8 will deliver better performance and is recommended. Another option is getting an ISDN card in your computer, along with an ISDN connection with your local phone company. Since this option isn't available everywhere, contact your local phone company to see if you can do it.

So, when you want to visit a Web page, you send a request to the specific Web server asking if you can download a particular Web page. The Web server then grants your request and sends the requested information.

An example of how SLIP connections help you can be seen by looking at Internet e-mail. A normal Internet e-mail account requires you to log on anytime you want and read your mail. Every time you log on, you spend time retrieving that information with your modem. If you use a SLIP e-mail account, all e-mail is automatically downloaded to your computer the first time you read it. You don't have to download the message every time you want to read it because it's already on your computer. This saves a lot of time in the long run.

History/Future of the Web

The Web has been around since early 1989, when a group of research scientists at CERN (The European Laboratory for Particle Physics in Switzerland) came up with the concept of how the Web would work. They released their work in 1991 and started generating interest in it. The scientists were significant in the set-up of the W3 Consortium, the powers that dictate the next generation of HTML and the Web.

After being used sparingly for about a year, Mosaic, the first extremely popular Web browser, was released and received rave reviews. Developed by the National Center for Supercomputing Applications (NCSA), Mosaic was easy to use, available on the UNIX, PC, and Macintosh platforms, and distributed freely. Not long after, the original developer of Mosaic partnered with Silicon Graphics to create Netscape, today's reigning browser software. It is estimated that as much as 80% of all Web traffic worldwide comes from people using Netscape. Like its predecessor, Netscape is free to single-users, and has been one of the leading pioneers in developing new Web technologies.

Since Mosaic was introduced, the Web has become exponentially more popular every year. In less then 4 years, the Web has surpassed every other popular Internet application including FTP, e-mail, and Gopher, to be the world's heaviest used piece of the Internet.

There are over 7 million Web pages to visit, each with its own unique content and identity.

Levels of HTML

When HTML, the underlying formatting language of the Web, was initially developed, it had limited functionality and text formatting characteristics. Since then, HTML has undergone a major revision, and the current standard is HTML 2.0.

Although HTML 2.0 offers quite a bit of flexibility to Web developers, it is only the beginning. Additional support for images, tables, and text formatting characteristics are in high demand. Web developers have long been asking for additional HTML support to enhance Web page graphic design and allow for more formatting control.

Fortunately, we're not far away from the next generation of HTML, version 3.0. Included in this next version, many new elements are added to give increased Web page flexibility.

Not waiting for HTML 3.0, Netscape announced their own enhancements to HTML, entitled the Netscape extensions. These extensions allow for increased text control and graphic support, almost everything that will be included with HTML 3.0, only available to use now.

This book teaches you how to take advantage of several Netscape Extensions. Most of these extensions will be included in HTML 3.0 in one form or another, and all of them will continue to be supported by future versions of Netscape. Because of Netscape's popularity, many sites create their Web pages especially for Netscape browsers to take advantage of these additional features.

What's a Home Page?

Think of a large city. There are commercial buildings, industrial buildings, and residences. Every building has its own unique identity, from large skyscrapers to fast food restaurants. They all have their own atmosphere and flavor. When you buy your own house, you get the opportunity to decorate and landscape it however you like. You can keep your house prim and proper with all the shrubs trimmed, or let weeds overtake your lawn.

Creating your own home page is a similar concept. There are thousands of home pages out there for businesses, organizations, and individuals. You're learning how to create your own home page, or residence on the World Wide Web. You get to choose what type of information and/or graphics to make available, how it looks when people stop by for a visit, and how to keep it properly maintained. A Web page that looks like garbage to you may be another's personal treasure trove.

There are no home page police that will stop by and make sure that everything is designed so that it's easy to use, or make sure the information on it is current. Your only restrictions are following the laws of your country (most notably, copyright, pornography, and privacy laws). It takes some effort to create an attractive and innovative home page that people will want to visit time and time again.

Read on to the next chapter to learn where and how to start building your own home page. You'll learn how to think through the home page process, how to sketch out and organize your page, and what tools will make it easier to construct your page.

Chapter 2

Starting to Weave Your Own Web

In the last chapter I gave an overview of the World Wide Web which included a brief explanation of a home page. Now you're ready to start learning how to create your own personal home page and make it available for the millions of people on the Internet to check out. This chapter covers:

- The kind of information you want to put on your home page
- How you might want your home page to look
- Netscape basics
- The easy-to-use Hotdog HTML editor
- Internet connections for establishing a home page

Why Create a Home Page?

There are over 7,000,000 (that's right, 6 zeros) Web pages out there already, and you are getting ready to mark your own corner of the Internet. Before you do, it's a good idea to decide *why* you want your own home page.

Home pages come in all different shapes and sizes. Some are merely personalized Internet vanity plates, while others offer unique information found nowhere else (such as the floating fish cam page—a home page that takes snapshots of an aquarium periodically through the day). Many people offer their services or sell products directly through their home pages.

Some people have Web pages just for fun, others just heard about the Web and thought a home page would be cool. You've got to decide your own reason for having a Web page.

> **Note**
>
> Personally, I think everyone should have their own Web page so they can create their own unique environment that reflects their personality. My Web page reflects my interests and lets others with the same interests interact with me.
>
> I don't have a Web page to sell my services or promote my products (although you can certainly find that information on there), instead I want that information to be freely available to whomever might want it.

Once you've decided *why* you want a home page, your next decision is *what* information should appear on it. Having an established home page goal will make it tremendously easier for you to design and create your Web page.

Personal Pages

The vast majority of Web pages out there are personal home pages, created by individuals just like you. Ironically, personal pages are the ones you are least likely to visit because:

There are so many of them and they aren't indexed by category

There aren't as cool as some of the impressive, commercial sites

However, personal home pages offer you your own customized place on the WWW and allow you to share information with your friends, family, and other Internet denizens.

Most of the information in this book is geared towards helping you create snazzy-looking personal Web pages. Here's a list of information that commonly appears on a personal home page:

- Contact Information
- Hobbies
- Interests
- Occupation
- Personal Background
- Self-Picture
- Publications
- Links to other neat Web pages

> **Tip**
>
> Many people create home pages and then put their URL on their business cards and resumes (I do). Not only does this demonstrate that they are technically savvy, but it also gives them a chance to let their true personality shine.

Business Pages

As more and more individuals are jumping onto the WWW, an increasing amount of businesses are also taking the plunge. Virtually every day a new large company or corporation is announcing their brand new site on the Web, and scores of smaller companies make their appearance as well.

Asked why they want to be on the Web, practically every company will answer the same thing—"It's a fantastic and complete marketing tool." The WWW offers an unprecedented opportunity for businesses and companies to get publicity and market their products and/or services for a relatively cheap price.

Support

Companies such as Microsoft, Lotus, and IBM have recognized the potential to offer technical support to their customers via the WWW. Microsoft offers a technical knowledge (see fig. 2.1) and Lotus has its internal "white papers" all available through the Web.

Supporting customers on the Web has evolved into an effective and affordable medium and more and more companies offer support over the Web every day.

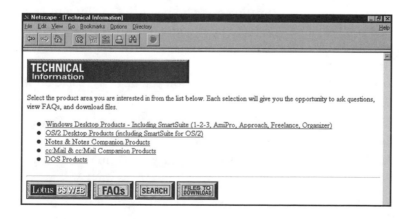

Fig. 2.1
Here's a sample of Microsoft's support site (**http:// www.microsoft. com/Support/**).

Sell Products

Nowadays, you can buy virtually anything on WWW. Whether you want an antique rocking chair, or clothing from the latest fashion, you'll find it on the Web (see fig. 2.2).

Apparently, selling products on the Web is quite lucrative. Several companies have announced that their sales have gone up significantly since they've had a presence on the WWW. The more you browse on the Web, the more you'll find an opportunity to spend money and buy items from the comfort of your own computer (You can even order a pizza through the Web in some places).

Fig. 2.2
Here's a good place to see how companies are selling their wares over the Web (**http://www.imall.com/homepage.html**).

Gathering Ideas and Constructing a Blueprint

There are two aspects to evaluating every home page: Content and Presentation. First you have to decide what information to put on your home page. Some people (like me) put personal information such as pictures and hobbies on their pages, while others only list their technical interests. You get to decide how much and what type of information you make available on the Web.

Don't worry if you can't decide exactly what to put on your home page. There are no wrong answers. Simply create your page, put it on the WWW, and see what other people think. The response you get from your original page will likely motivate you for updating it in various ways.

Read this section to learn about different ways of organizing and presenting your home page. You'll see several different home pages that actually exist, and some suggestions for how you can make your page top-notch. While I won't tell you what exactly to put on your home page, I will make some suggestions and show you some examples to help you along the way. As I do, I'll point out some of the good things you may want to include and some of the bad things you may want to avoid.

Short but Sweet—Roxanne's Page

This page is an example of how even an extremely simple home page can easily fit your needs, represent yourself adequately, and not take an overwhelming amount of time designing, planning, and maintaining.

Take a look at Roxanne's page (see fig. 2.3). She lists a few things that are important to her—taxes, coin collecting, and her cockatiel. What's great about this page is that it is easy to read and well presented.

Stop by and visit her at **http://www.geopages.com/CapitolHill/1099/**.

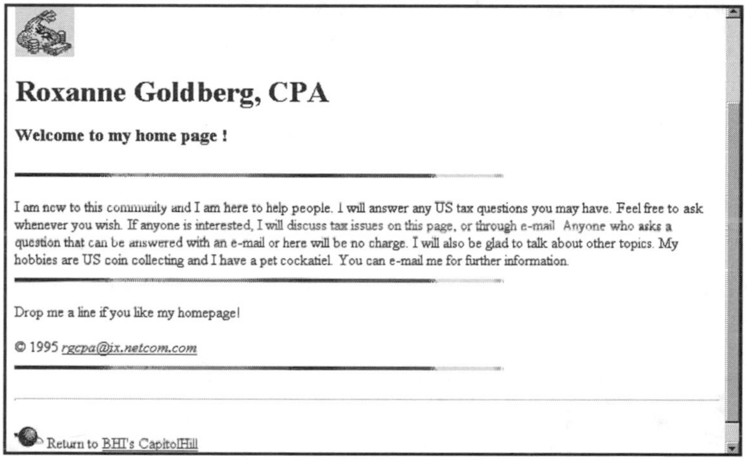

Fig. 2.3
Roxanne's Page is easy to take care of, but there's not a lot of meat there (yet).

Intermediate Level—My Personal Page

Here's my own personal home page (see fig. 2.4). You might be surprised that it doesn't have thousands of graphics, tons of links, and use every Netscape feature listed in this book. I have spent a lot of time organizing my page to make it easy to use. I've also discovered that most pages that have an abundance of graphics are often too confusing to even use.

That said, my page is the next level up from Roxanne's in difficulty, design, and presentation. It took me a while to put together, but isn't that difficult to keep current or add new information. My URL is: **http://www.cis.ohio-state.edu/~shafran/**.

Fig. 2.4
My page represents an organized home page without adding too many z's to pizzazz.

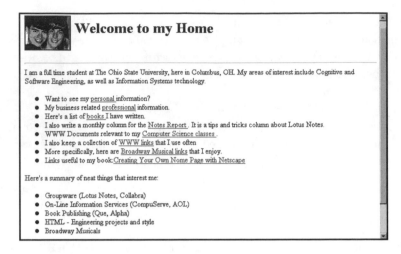

Classy Web Page—The Crime Scene

This is one of my favorite sites on the WWW. This is the home page for an ongoing investigation regarding a murder that occurred in Mississippi (everything is fictional—honest).

This site uses a nice combination of text, graphics, and organizational techniques for an all-around superb site. Exploring this site you'll find video clips, audio bites, and several images all related to the case.

Visit **http://odin.cbu.edu/~vaskin/crime/crime.html** to see if you can crack the case (see fig. 2.5)!

Fig. 2.5
The Crime Scene Evidence File is probably a precursor to how investigators may work in the future!

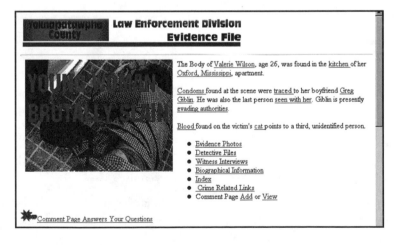

Excellent Commercial Site—ESPN SportsZone

I've included a couple of commercial sites so you could see what other types of pages look like. Commercial pages tend to be more impressive because they have more financial backing than individual home pages.

This site is ESPN's home page, titled **SportsZone** (see fig. 2.6). SportsZone offers an attractive format without any difficult to maintain HTML tricks. Every time you link to this page you find the newest and latest sports information. That makes you want to come back again and again.

Although their page design is simple, the large amount of information that constantly hits this page makes it one of the hottest spots on the Internet. Stop by and see for yourself at **http://espnet.sportszone.com/**.

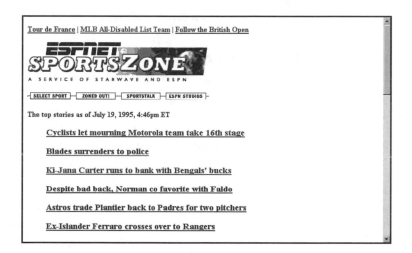

Fig. 2.6
ESPN's SportsZone talks about teams, trades, and tribulations affecting major league sports.

Fantastic Commercial Site—Coca-Cola

This is the place to stop by for a cool and interactive Web experience. One stop here and you know you're in for a treat (see fig. 2.7).

This site takes advantage of some of the most complicated features of Web Publishing. Geared towards Netscape, the site uses clickable graphics (where different spots of a graphic take you to different Web Pages), Forms, and practices good design techniques.

One drawback to creating a site like Coca-Cola is the amount of work it takes to maintain the Web Site. Updates constantly have to be created and the information always needs to stay current. In addition, creating the maps and forms used can be a difficult process even for programmers. But when you're a company as wealthy as Coca-Cola, you can afford it. Quench your thirst at **http://www.cocacola.com/**.

Fig. 2.7
It's fun looking at sites like this, but maintaining it would be a nightmare.

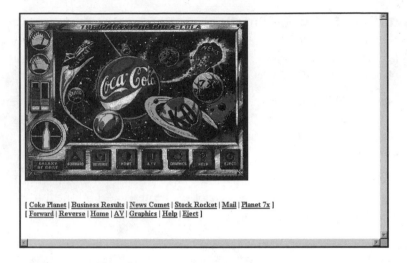

Organizing your Home Page

After finishing the whirlwind tour of the above Web sites, you probably have lots of ideas for what you want to put on your home page. Before you dive in, though, you may want to take a few minutes to think about what you're going to include. Just as an architect doesn't build without a blueprint, neither should you design a Web page without first figuring out what belongs where.

The first step is organizing the information you want to put on your page. I recommend organizing your home page into three different categories—personal, professional, and miscellaneous. After all, your goal is to put useful information about yourself on the WWW.

Now when visitors stop by your home page, they know where to look for information. Friends can go to the personal section, potential employers know that the professional section is what they want, and everyone can explore your miscellaneous section. If everything was just listed together, visitors have to read through your entire page before they find what they're looking for.

Then you'll need to break down each section even further. Decide whether you want to make your address and phone number available. Do you want to include a picture of yourself? What kinds of hobbies do you have? Visit my home page to see how I dealt with those issues. Feel free to "borrow" design ideas from my page or any other page that you like on the Internet.

> **Tip**
>
> Remember that you don't have to put **everything** on your home page on the first try. Spend your time putting a good but simple (Roxanne's) page up there first. From there you can increase your page's complexity.

Sketching your Page Out

Once you've started organizing your information, take some time sketching out how you want your home page to look. Just because the WWW is on a computer doesn't mean that good old pencil and paper can't help you out.

Draw your ideal page. Put your images, lines of text, and headlines all on your sheet of paper. I've found that drawing out Web pages (called prototyping in the business world) helps me think through the whole process. I know how big I want to make my images, how much text to type (approximately), what colors (if any) to use, and what kind of tables and lists I need to use (you'll learn more about these in chapter 4). Don't be afraid to draw several sketches, even if they are very different (see fig. 2.8).

By adding this step to your Web page process, you're bound to have put more thought into what information makes sense on a home page and how you want to present it.

Fig. 2.8
Here are a few sketches of how I thought my home page could look.

Show Your Home Page with Netscape

As I said in the last chapter, Netscape is the world's most popular browser. I use Netscape exclusively through this book to browse the WWW and my personal HTML documents. Not only is Netscape extremely easy to use and efficient at navigating the Web, it also supports special extensions, or enhancements, to the current standard of HTML.

Using these extensions you have significantly more control over the way your home page looks. I thoroughly cover the Netscape extensions in this book along with other HTML features.

This means that the home pages you create should be viewed with Netscape to get the full effect. Since Netscape is free, this shouldn't pose a problem to you. In this section, I'll show you where and how to download and install Netscape.

To go to Netscape, click on the big "N" in the top right corner (**http://home.netscape.com/**).

 Back—Clicking on this button takes you to the most previously viewed Web page.

 Forward—Clicking on this button takes you to the next page you viewed (usually used after clicking on the **Back** button).

 Home—Clicking on this button takes you to the home page as defined in your Netscape Preferences.

 Reload—Clicking this button requests the current Web page you're viewing to be loaded again.

 Images—Clicking this button tells Netscape to reload all of the images on the current Web page.

 Open—Clicking on this button opens a dialog box that let's you open a new URL.

 Print—Clicking this button will print the current Web page.

 Find—Clicking this button will open a dialog box that will let you search for words on the current Web page.

 Stop—While Netscape is loading a Web page, clicking on this button will stop the process.

Downloading and Installing Netscape

When this book was written, the latest version of Netscape was version 1.2, but you'll want to double-check and see if a later version is available. If you aren't running Netscape, or have an older version, follow these steps to download the newest version.

On the Web, go to **http://home.netscape.com/comprod/mirror/index.html**. From here you can navigate and download the latest version directly to your computer. This download can take a while depending on your modem speed (20-25 minutes at 14.4 baud).

> **Tip**
>
> If you don't have Netscape yet, or would prefer to FTP Netscape to your computer, then FTP to **ftp://ftp.netscape.com/pub/**; you can download the file from there. Please note, however, that when using some ftp programs (such as WS_FTP) you do not have to include the ftp:// portion of the address, so you would simply use **ftp.netscape.com**.

Once Netscape is downloaded to your machine, use the Windows File Manager to run the self-executable file. Follow the installation instructions to install Netscape on your computer's hard drive.

Remember that you must have a working SLIP or PPP Internet account using a WinSock client (If this is gibberish to you, contact your Internet provider, or see chapter 1) for Netscape to work properly.

> **Note**
>
> To run Netscape 1.2 (and higher) with Windows 95, use the built-in Internet software to connect to your Internet provider. The WinSock client that you used under Windows 3.1 won't work under Windows 95 (although your other Internet applications should work—FTP, Trumpet, and your e-mail package). Since Windows 95 has built-in PPP support, you shouldn't need one, however. Netscape is available in a 32-bit version designed specifically for Windows 95 and Windows NT. If you use Windows 3.X, you must use the 16-bit version.

Innovative Features

Netscape's Extensions allow home page designers like yourself additional flexibility when it comes to creating your Web pages. With the built-in extensions you get:

- Additional image placement support

- Control over the length and width of Horizontal Rules

- More font size control

- Full table support and integration into home pages

- Control over background colors and/or images

- Extra text format tags such as <BLINK> and <CENTER>

Double-Check your Home Page with Another Browser

Using Netscape as the primary browser does have one significant drawback. Netscape's HTML extensions do not work with other WWW browsers. Advanced image formatting and table tags may look great with Netscape but could resemble a jumbled mess in another browser.

Although Netscape is significantly more popular than other browsers, it is always a good idea to see how your home page looks with another non-Netscape browser. For all of the neat Netscape features you can use, you want your home page to be accessible to anyone who wants to browse it.

If you want to see your home page from another set of eyes, use the following table to locate and download other WWW browsers.

Other popular WWW Browsers and their URLs (visit Yahoo)	
Mosaic	Developed at CERN, the original Web browser is similar to Netscape Address: **http://www.ncsa.uiuc.edu/SDG/Software/ SDGSoftDir.html**
Lynx	This is a text-based browser for those on workstations or in non-graphical environments Address: **http://www.cc.ukans.edu/ about_lynx/about_lynx.html**
Arena	A browser designed to test new HTML standards currently on runs in UNIX Address: **http://www.w3.org/hypertext/WWW/ Arena/**

Write HTML with Hotdog

As I discussed in chapter 1, HTML Documents are text-based files that have special codes, called markup tags, within them. These markup tags instruct

WWW browsers such as Netscape how to interpret and display text and graphics.

Since HTML documents are completely text, virtually any word processor or text editor from Windows Notepad to WordPerfect can be used to create a home page. The difficult part about creating HTML documents is remembering all the specific markup tags and learning how to use them properly.

Several programs exist to make it easier to create HTML documents. In this book, I use one of the best, Hotdog. Hotdog is Shareware software that allows you to create incredible looking WWW documents without knowing very much about HTML. You simply type in the text to appear on your home page and use Hotdog's buttons to mark how text should appear. You can even preview how your document will appear directly in Netscape. Hotdog also provides many of the same functions as a standard word processor.

Tip

Shareware programs are software packages that you are permitted to evaluate and use for free for a limited period of time. After that evaluation period is over (usually around 30 days), you must purchase the program to legally continue using it.

Included on the CD-ROM in the back of this book, Hotdog makes it easy for you to create your own home page. Hotdog is geared towards creating effective looking HTML documents that take advantage of the Netscape extensions.

Tip

The version of Hotdog included on the home page CD is a Shareware version which is only good for 30 days. To use Hotdog after that, you can buy the Standard edition for $29.95. Soon to be released, Hotdog Professional Edition is a full-blown impressive HTML editor that allows you to customize your Hotdog icon bar, comes with several HTML templates, and may even support Java and VRML (see chapter 9 for more information on those). The Hotdog professional edition will cost you $79.95. Either way, stop by the Hotdog home page at http://www.sausage.com for more information.

Read the next section to learn how to install and the basics of using Hotdog to create your home page.

Installing the Hotdog HTML Editor

Hotdog version 1.0 can be found on the included CD-ROM. Simply insert the CD in your drive and do the following:

For Windows 3.1 select the File menu title and the Run menu item.

For Windows 95 select the Start button choose the Run item.

Type **D:\EDITORS\HOTDOG\SETUP.EXE** and hit return. Make sure to replace the D drive with the drive letter for your CD-ROM.

Hotdog will walk you through the installation process and set itself up on your hard drive. Once installed, Hotdog allows you 30 days of free use until your license expires.

Once Hotdog is installed on your computer, you've got to customize it so it can use Netscape to preview your HTML documents. From the menu bar, choose Tools, Options to bring up the Options dialog box. Click on the tab labeled File Locations to set your Hotdog options (shown in fig. 2.10). In the Preview Browser box type in the full filename and extension of where Netscape resides on your computer. For my computer, it's on the D drive in the Netscape directory.

Once you've typed in the full path name and directory, click on the Save Options button. Hotdog is now linked to your Netscape browser (see fig. 2.9).

Fig. 2.9
Give Hotdog a roadmap to find Netscape on your hard drive.

Tip

Several other good HTML editors are included on the home page CD in this book. If you have extra time, take a few minutes to browse through and evaluate some of the others.

Make sure you stop by the Hotdog home page at **HTTP://
www.sausage.com** to see if a newer version of Hotdog is available for
download (see fig. 2.10).

Fig. 2.10
The Hotdog home
page is fun and
whimsical to
visit and is the
clearinghouse for
future releases of
the editor.

A Brief Hotdog Tour

Once Hotdog is installed on Windows 3.1, double-click on the icon labeled
"Hotdog Editor" to begin the program. To run Hotdog from Windows 95 you
have to use the File Explorer (or use the Find option) to locate the Hotdog
program. Once you find it, double-click the Hotdog program to start up the
editor. A Shareware notice appears, and then the main editor window appears. The first time you use Hotdog, a dialog box will come up asking you
for your next action. Click on the Use Hotdog Now button to continue (see
fig.2.11).

Tip

If you're using Windows 95 and Hotdog a lot, you might want to create a shortcut
for it. To create this shortcut, simply locate the Hotdog program and click the right
mouse button. From the pop-up menu select "Create Shortcut." A shortcut to the
Hotdog editor will appear on the desktop, so you can run it whenever you feel like
and not look around for it.

Fig. 2.11

Here's the main Hotdog screen ready to go!

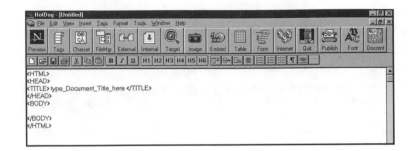

Preview—Click on this button to see a preview of your current HTML document in Netscape.

Tags—Click on this button to choose from a number of drag-and-drop HTML tags.

Charset—Click on this button to choose from a number of drag-and-drop special character formats such as bold.

FileMgr—Click on this button to access the Hotdog File manager, from which you can retrieve HTML, image and other documents from your hard drive.

External—Click on this button to link your home page to other documents on the WWW.

Internal—Click on this button to link highlighted text to specific targets in your home page.

Target—Click on this button to create targets in your home page that you can link to (useful when you have a big home page).

Image—Click on this button to create an inline image.

Embed—Click on this button to choose a file to embed as a link within your document.

Table—Click on this button to create a table within your HTML document.

Form—Click on this button to add form elements to your document.

Internet—Click on this button to insert hypertext links for Internet functions such as e-mail or FTP.

Quit—Click on this button to quit Hotdog.

 Publish—Click on this button to save your document and apply any special publishing options on your text that you set (tools, options).

 Font—Click this button to add formatting to your document text.

 Document—Click on this button to set document-wide attributes such as background color.

You'll use the buttons lining the top of the screen to add new HTML elements to your home page. All you have to do is type your home page information in the main window. Then, using your mouse, highlight the different parts of the text you want add an HTML tag to. Click on the appropriate button and voilà, your text is marked automatically.

For example, type in the following text in your main window:

> Extra! Extra! Read all about it!
>
> According to Fortune Magazine, Bill Gates is the second richest person in the world, second only to royalty who inherited his money from his family and past generations. Not to be outdone, Gates intends to buy his own country and set himself up as monarch for life.

Now take your mouse and highlight "Fortune Magazine." We want to italicize that text because it is a magazine's title. So click on the Italics button and watch Hotdog add the <I> and </I> tags automatically for you. Now boldface Gates' name wherever it appears in the preceding paragraph by selecting the text and clicking on the boldface icon. Finally, let's make the first line look like a headline. Select it and click on the **H1** button.

When you are finished, your text should look like this:

```
<H1> Extra! Extra! Read all about it! </H1>

According to <I>Fortune Magazine </I>, <B>Bill Gates </B> is the
second richest person in the world, second only to royalty who
inherited his money from his family and past generations. Not to be
outdone, <B>Gates</B> intends to buy his own country and set him-
self up as monarch for life.
```

Now click on the Netscape **Preview** button. Netscape appears and shows you how the text would look to people browsing on the Web (see fig. 2.12).

Fig. 2.12
Not too compli-
cated, but pretty
neat for ten
seconds of work.

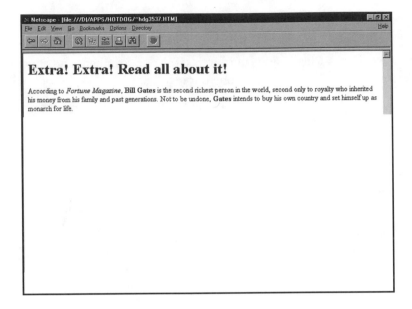

Connecting to a Web Provider

Once you have Netscape and Hotdog in place, the last piece of "equipment" you'll need to create your own home page is a spot on the Internet.

A Web provider is someone who rents space on their computer connected to the Internet for a monthly fee. For this small charge, you can put your own customized home page on the Internet and let it be available to anyone across the world any time they wish to stop by.

You probably already have an Internet provider if you're already browsing the Web. Many Internet providers double as Web providers and allow you to put your home page up. However, some Internet providers don't offer this type of access and others charge an arm and a leg.

This section describes the ideal characteristics of a Web provider and even offers some pointers to finding your own spot on the Internet.

What You are Looking for

Web providers come in all different shapes and sizes. Some of them are friendly and affordable while others charge outrageous fees and add hidden costs at every turn. Here is a list of characteristics of a good Web provider:

- **Freedom**—You can have anything you want on your home page (assuming it doesn't break any laws).

- **Reliability**—Your home page is useless if the provider's Web site is unreliable. Stop by their home page several times during peak (day) and non-peak (evening) hours to make sure you have no problems accessing their site.

- **Affordability**—After doing comparison shopping, you're being ripped off if you pay more than $10 a month for your home page. In fact I've even found some sites that offer free Web pages to anyone who asks (read on for those).

- **Support**—Web page publishing can be difficult if no one is there to answer your questions. This book should guide you through most of your basic HTML questions, but you're bound to have more.

- **Creativity**—The more people that visit your Web provider's site, the more people that could stop by your home page. Your Web provider's home page is often an accurate gauge for how much they know HTML and how creative they are.

Expected Costs

As I mentioned above, you can find a good Web provider that will charge you under $10 a month for storing a decent size Web page at their Internet site.

Several other costs can be accrued when creating a new Web site. Most of these can be avoided, but be aware that these extra costs can nickel-and-dime you until you're in the poorhouse—if you're not careful.

- Startup Costs—Ranging from $0 to $150, Web providers often charge a one time fee to set up and install your personal Web page. After buying this book, you shouldn't need to pay anyone an extra dime for setting up a Web page—you'll know almost as much as they do.

- Maintenance Charges—A good Web page will have information updated often. Some Web providers let you update your page for free, others charge as much as $50 for ongoing maintenance. I try to stick only with the free ones, but keep your eyes peeled.

- Consulting Charges—Most Web providers also offer customized Web consulting to create advanced Web pages for businesses and companies. If advanced and complicated HTML publishing is what you need (like the Coca-Cola page seen earlier this chapter), expect to pay at least $50 an hour.

Pointer to Appendix

I've included a list of quality Web providers that offer extremely affordable Web pages to any WWW users. Their prices range from free to $10 a month, and they all have their own strengths and disadvantages.

Check out appendix A for my list of affordable and friendly Web providers.

One Alternative: Running Your Own Web Server

Another alternative to renting Internet space from a Web provider is setting up and creating your own WWW server on the Internet. With significant startup and monthly maintenance charges, this option is for the truly Web-dedicated companies out there.

For more information on how to setup and run a Web server, check out the book *Running a Perfect Web Site* also published by Que.

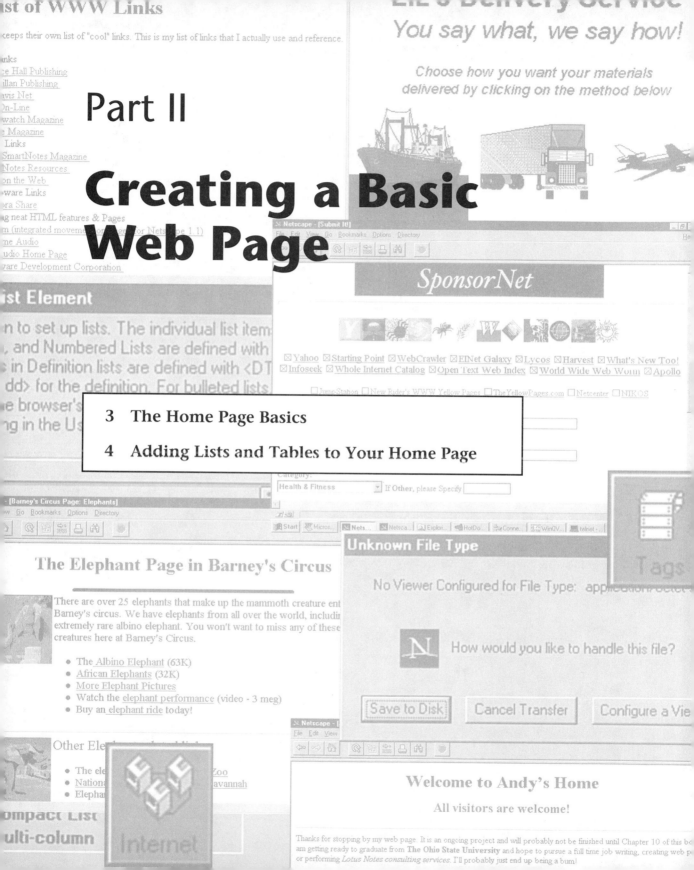

Part II

Creating a Basic Web Page

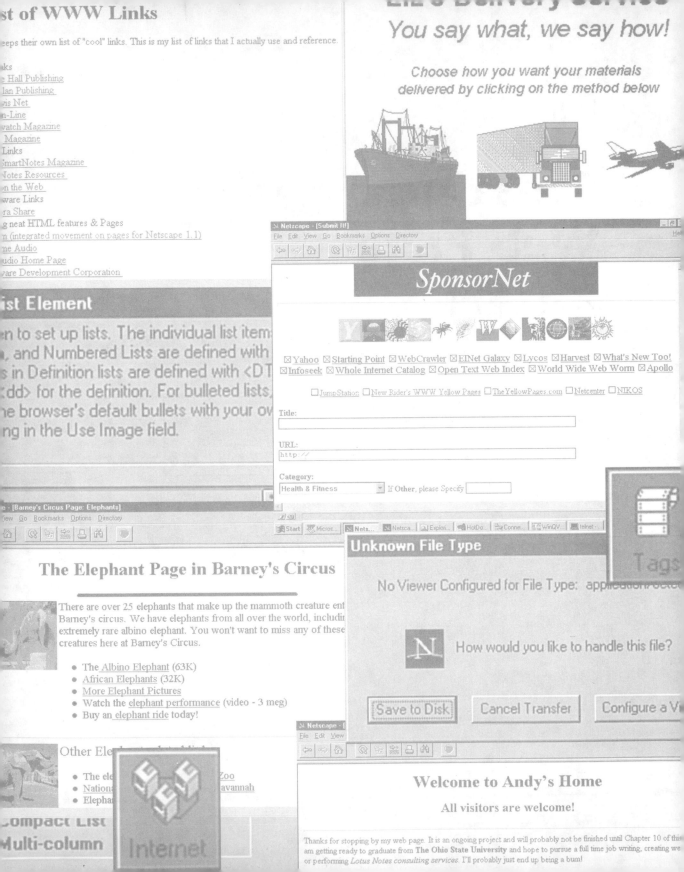

st of WWW Links

eeps their own list of "cool" links. This is my list of links that I actually use and reference.

ks
e Hall Publishing
lan Publishing
is Net
n-Line
vatch Magazine
Magazine
Links
SmartNotes Magazine
Notes Resources
n the Web
ware Links
ra Share
g neat HTML features & Pages
n (integrated movement on pages for Netscape 1.1)
ne Audio
udio Home Page
vare Development Corporation

ist Element

n to set up lists. The individual list item
, and Numbered Lists are defined with
s in Definition lists are defined with <DT
<dd> for the definition. For bulleted lists,
ne browser's default bullets with your ow
ng in the Use Image field.

You say what, we say how!

Choose how you want your materials
delivered by clicking on the method below

Netscape - [Submit It!]
File Edit View Go Bookmarks Options Directory

SponsorNet

☒Yahoo ☒Starting Point ☒WebCrawler ☒EINet Galaxy ☒Lycos ☒Harvest ☒What's New Too!
☒Infoseek ☒Whole Internet Catalog ☒Open Text Web Index ☒World Wide Web Worm ☒Apollo

☐JumpStation ☐New Rider's WWW Yellow Pages ☐TheYellowPages.com ☐Netcenter ☐NIKOS

Title:

URL:
http://

Category:
Health & Fitness ▾ If Other, please Specify

Start | Micro... | Nets... | Netsca | Explori | HotDo.. | Conne.. | WinQV | telnet -

e - [Barney's Circus Page: Elephants]
iew Go Bookmarks Options Directory

The Elephant Page in Barney's Circus

There are over 25 elephants that make up the mammoth creature ent
Barney's circus. We have elephants from all over the world, includir
extremely rare albino elephant. You won't want to miss any of these
creatures here at Barney's Circus.

- The Albino Elephant (63K)
- African Elephants (32K)
- More Elephant Pictures
- Watch the elephant performance (video - 3 meg)
- Buy an elephant ride today!

Other Ele   Zoo
- The ele
- Nationa   vannah
- Elepha

Unknown File Type

No Viewer Configured for File Type: appliсation/octer

How would you like to handle this file?

Save to Disk   Cancel Transfer   Configure a V

Netscape -
File Edit View

Welcome to Andy's Home

All visitors are welcome!

Thanks for stopping by my web page. It is an ongoing project and will probably not be finished until Chapter 10 of thi
am getting ready to graduate from **The Ohio State University** and hope to pursue a full time job writing, creating we
or performing *Lotus Notes consulting services*. I'll probably just end up being a bum!

ompact List
Multi-column   Internet

Chapter 3

The Home Page Basics

HTML isn't a complicated language to learn, but there are some quirks. In fact, most HTML is intuitive and easy to read. When you go to England, the people there speak English but have their own vernacular colloquialisms. Although it's not quite as easy as speaking British English, you won't have to learn an entirely new language (like Russian) to create a good home page.

I spent the last couple of chapters introducing the WWW and helping you get ready to create your home page. You saw several different types of home pages, learned the basics about the tools I use in this book, and learned how to find a Web provider.

Now that you're finished with the planning stages of your Web page, let's start making it! In this chapter, you'll learn how to:

- Use important standard tags that are in every home page

- Enlarge specific text to serve as a headline

- Separate your text into paragraphs and easy to read chunks

- Bold face, italicize, and center text

Using the Standard Home Page Template

I have included a sample home page template on the CD that comes with this book. This sample template contains tags preformatted for a simple, but elegant home page. All you need to do is add your own text! My home page uses the same template.

Web Pages

Feel free to use, customize, and modify the home page template to your heart's desire. It's meant to be flexible to your needs, not rigid.

Although the template is included, I don't spend much time using it in this book. Instead, I show you how to use Hotdog to markup text from scratch. You'll learn how I built the template, how to use HTML tags, and what design decisions I've made.

Important HTML Tags

No matter what your page looks like or what kind of information you want to display, there are four HTML tags that every page should have so they follow HTML and WWW standards.

- <HTML>—Informs the browser that this document is written in HTML.
- <HEAD>—Labels the introductory and heading part of the HTML document.
- <BODY>—Marks where the body text and information appears.
- <ADDRESS>—Contains an e-mail address to get further information about this web page.

These tags are vital to telling your Web browser (notably Netscape) how to recognize different parts of the HTML document, but they don't affect how your home page appears. They're necessary for future enhancements of HTML to be able to use your home page properly. For example, your Web server might run a program that looks at every HTML document and tries to create a large listing of them all. It might only list the text that appears in the <HEAD> tag because that's where the title of the document should go. So, if your home page doesn't use the <HEAD> and </HEAD> tags, you wouldn't be included in the listing. In general, while they don't affect how your home page looks, using these tags is considered proper.

Note

By default, WWW pages created with Netscape automatically have the <HTML>, <HEAD>, and <BODY> tags in them. You'll have to add the <ADDRESS> tag yourself.

<HTML> and </HTML>

This tag is important because it tells browsers to interpret the text inside of these tags as HTML text. Since HTML documents are strictly text based, the <HTML> tag lets you know that a file is written in Hypertext Markup Language.

To use these tags, put the tag **<HTML>** at the very top of your file. It should be the first typed text on your screen. Then type in its companion tag **</HTML>** at the very end of the file. All the text surrounded by these tags are now marked as written in HTML format. Did you notice the "/" in the second tag? The forward slash is used to indicate ending HTML tags. Most HTML tags come in pairs, surrounding the text they markup. The closing tag of a pair will always start with a forward slash.

So far, your home page looks like this:

```
<HTML>

</IITML>
```

<HEAD> and </HEAD>

The next set of tags you want to include is the <HEAD> and </HEAD> tags. These tags identify and mark information in your HTML document that serves as the document's header, or title information.

Adding these tags to your home page is just as easy as the <HTML> tags. Type **<HEAD>** on the screen in between the <HTML> tags and then type in its companion tag, **</HEAD>**, on the following line.

<BODY> and </BODY>

Just like the <HEAD> tags, you use <BODY> and </BODY> to delineate a separate part of your HTML document. Text surrounded by the <BODY> tags represents the main meat of a document.

This is where most of your text and information will be typed because they are part of the document's body. Add **<BODY>** and **</BODY>** to your home page and now your entire document looks like this (I added the tabs to make it easier to read):

<ADDRESS> and </ADDRESS>

We've added three sets of tags to your home page, but no text. Now we'll add the <ADDRESS> tags, and this time we'll use Hotdog to create the tags. The <ADDRESS> tags contain information about who to contact regarding this particular page. It is important to always put some kind of contact information on a web page in case someone has a question or comment they want to ask you.

The <ADDRESS> tag is used to separate that important information from the regular text body. Follow these steps to add the <ADDRESS> tag to your home page.

1. In between the <BODY> and </BODY> tags, type your name and e-mail address like this:

   Andy Shafran—shafran@cis.ohio-state.edu

2. Using your mouse, highlight the text you just typed and click on the **Tags** button to bring up the available tags window (see fig. 3.1).

Fig. 3.1
HTML tags that you can drag onto your home page are listed here.

3. Double-click your mouse on the **Address** tag. Hotdog automatically adds the <ADDRESS> and </ADDRESS> tags for you around your text.

Tip

You can also drag and drop tags directly onto your home page.

Look at figure 3.2 to see the HTML on your home page.

Fig. 3.2
Here's my home page in Hotdog so far.

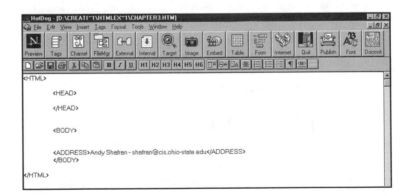

Tip

You could also use the Hotdog Tag editor to add the <HTML>, <HEAD>, and <BODY> tags if you want.

Caution

Even though you're just getting started, save your HTML file now with the **File**, **Save** command. Save frequently and regularly so you don't accidentally lose your work. When you save, your file name appears in the Hotdog title bar.

Titling Your Home Page

Now that your basic four HTML tags are created on your home page, you can start adding some text to your page. Let's start by adding a title to your home page with the <TITLE> and </TITLE> tags.

The home page title is displayed in the Netscape title bar when you are browsing that page. Additionally, it is the page's title that is saved in Netscape's bookmark list of web pages you like to visit.

Your title belongs within the <HEAD> and </HEAD> tags on your home page. You can only have one title per HTML document. Type in your home page's title between the <HEAD> and </HEAD> tags. Highlight it with your mouse and use the **Tags** button in Hotdog to mark it as a title. Scroll though the list of tags and drag **Title** onto your home page from the tags box. Your HTML should look like this:

<TITLE>Andy Shafran's home page</TITLE>

Now click on the **Preview** button from Hotdog to bring up Netscape with your address information (see fig. 3.3).

Here's where the title appears in Netscape

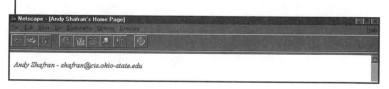

Fig. 3.3
Your title is an important label for your home page.

Make sure you type a short, to the point, and informative title.

> **Tip**
>
> Bad home page titles are wordy, lengthy, and uninformative.

Titles should fit within the Netscape title bar, be easy to reference, and accurately describe the site they represent. Good home page titles include:

Andy Shafran's Home Page

Shafran's Web Page

Andy's Web Site

Visiting Andy's Page

Some bad home page title examples are:

My Page

This is the fantastic, wonderful place to visit on the Web where Andy Shafran's home page resides

Home Page, Sweet Home Page

Creating Headlines

Once your title is in place, your next step is to add a headline that will appear on your Web page. Headlines are similar to titles in that they should be succinct and useful. Headlines come in six different sizes, (creatively numbered one through six, with one being the largest). Figure 3.4 shows how the different headline sizes look in Netscape.

Fig. 3.4
Here's how the six different headline sizes stack up against each other.

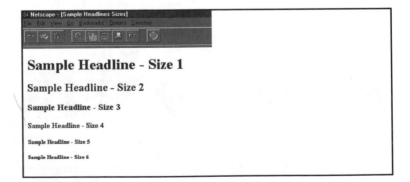

In Netscape they appear larger and bolder than standard text and are a great way to delineate different parts of your Web page.

To use a size 1 headline on your home page, you would use the <H1> and </H1> HTML tags around the text you want to mark. Try adding a headline to your current page. Make sure that your text falls within the <BODY> and </BODY> tags.

1. Type your headline text onto your Web page:

    Welcome to Andy's Home

2. Highlight your text with your mouse.

3. Click on the button labeled **H1** in the smaller Hotdog icon bar at the top of the screen. Headline tags appear and automatically surround your text:

    <H1>Welcome to Andy's Home</H1>

4. Adding a secondary headline is just as easy. On the next line after your level 1 headline, type a secondary line of information, highlight it, and click on the **H2** button:

    <H2>All visitors are welcome!</H2>

5. Click on the **Preview** button to see your home page in Netscape (see fig. 3.5).

Fig. 3.5
Here's how Netscape sees my home page, headlines and all.

II

Creating Web Pages

You'll add headlines of all sizes to your home page. I use headlines to organize the different sub-sections of my home page. As a general rule of design, if you use two headlines right after each other, only change the headline level by one increment (go from level 1 to level 2, or level 3 to level 4). This makes the transition from one level of text to the next appear natural to the eye.

Adding Text and Information

With your home page properly titled and headlined, let's add some more information that tells your visitors about yourself. Adding text to your home page is arguably the easiest step in the home page creation process because you can type directly into Hotdog and it will appear as normal text when viewing it with Netscape.

I'm going to add a paragraph about myself to my sample Web page that I've been working on all chapter:

> Thanks for stopping by my web page. It is an ongoing project and will probably not be finished until chapter 11 of this book. My personal interests include learning about computers, reading, and watching Broadway musicals. I am getting ready to graduate from The Ohio State University and hope to pursue a full time job writing, creating Web pages, or performing Lotus Notes consulting services. I'll probably just end up being a bum!

After typing that text, I can hit the **Preview** button to see how it looks in Netscape (see fig. 3.6). I can change my text and save my home page when I am finished.

Fig. 3.6

Here's how all the text comes out in Netscape.

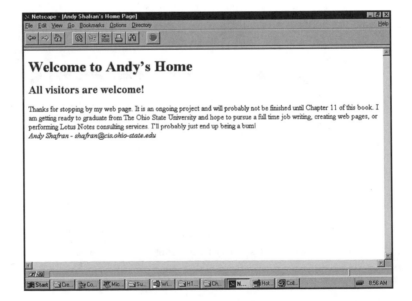

Breaking Text into Readable Chunks

Once you start adding text to your home page, you'll soon realize that Netscape doesn't display your text exactly how you type it onto your home page. For example, the following text appears like this when typing it into Hotdog:

Here's a list of things I like to do in my spare time:

- Read books

- Travel

- Surf the Internet

- Enjoy live theater

But it looks quite different when browsing it with Netscape (see fig. 3.7).

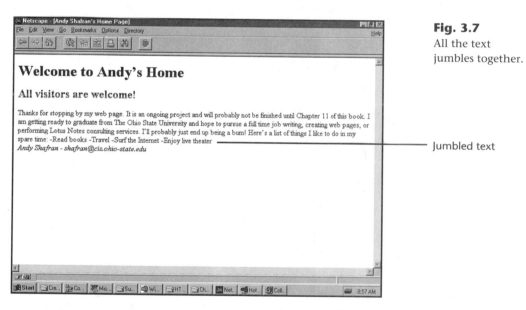

Fig. 3.7
All the text
jumbles together.

Jumbled text

That's because Netscape only formats information according to your markup tags. HTML is a *formatting language* and tells browsers such as Netscape what to do with text. If you think the above example was jumbled, think of a large block of text that includes several different paragraphs. Since Netscape ignores white space between paragraphs, you'd only see one huge block of text!

II

Creating Web Pages

Caution

Netscape ignores spaces, tabs, and line breaks between text unless you define them with the correct markup tags.

The following sections introduce you to some of the basic text placement markup tags. You'll learn how to break up your text into readable bits using the paragraph and line break tags, as well as work with the horizontal rule—a line that is drawn across the screen to separate pieces of text.

Unlike most tags, these tags do not appear in pairs. Netscape recognizes the single tags and spaces your text accordingly.

Paragraph Tag

The paragraph tag (<P>) tells Netscape to separate two paragraphs of information with a blank line between them. It's useful when you have many paragraphs of text in a row.

Adding a paragraph tag is simple in Hotdog. Place your cursor in the spot you want to have a tag and click on the **dbutton**. A <P> tag is inserted automatically.

Tip

You don't have to use the paragraph tag to separate headlines, lists, and horizontal rules from text. By definition, Netscape automatically includes an extra line of space before and after those HTML elements.

Line Break Tag

The line break tag <BR> is similar to the paragraph tag, except that it does not add an extra line between the text it separates. After the tag, text continues directly at the beginning of the next line.

With Hotdog, you can add the <BR> tag by moving your cursor to the connect position and clicking on the <BR> button at the top of the screen.

I use the line break tag when I am creating a short list of items:

> <H3>My Favorite Musicals, in order:</H3>
>
> Les Miserables
>
> Jeckyll & Hyde

Cats

Pippin <P>

I used the <P> tag at the end of my list to separate the end of my list from the next paragraph (see fig. 3.8).

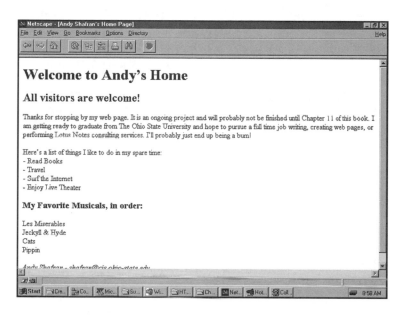

Fig. 3.8
My favorite musicals, Netscapized.

You add the line break tag the same way as the paragraph tag. Move your cursor to the correct position and click on the **line break button.**

> **Note**
>
> Netscape also supports the word break tag <WOBR>. Rarely used, the word break tag allows you to definitively split up words onto two separate lines. Just select **Word Break** from the list of available tags after clicking on the **Tags** button in Hotdog.

Web Pages

Horizontal Rules

The horizontal rule tag, <HR>, is one of the most useful and elegant tags available to help you separate and break up your home page.

Adding this tag to your HTML document creates a line that goes across the screen when using Netscape. This line is useful for logically separating different parts of your home page from each other.

I use the horizontal rule tag as an organizational and design tool. It helps people who view my Web page understand which pieces are related to each other, and it also separates my page into different pieces. For example, I use the <HR> tag right above my e-mail address on my Web page to split that information apart from the regular text on my home page.

You can use the <HR> tag anywhere within your HTML document's body. To add a horizontal rule tag, click on the **HR icon** in Hotdog's menu to bring up the horizontal rule dialog box. Click on the **OK button** to insert a standard line that runs completely across the page as shown in figure 3.9.

Fig. 3.9
I use the <HR> tag
to keep my page
ship-shape.

Netscapes <HR> Extensions

Bored with the standard <HR> tag, Netscape decided to spice up what you could do with the horizontal rule. They realized that a thin line across the page is useful in some cases, but occasionally you might want to have a different type of line. So they came up with a method for customizing how long your line is, how thick of a line displays, and how your line is aligned when viewing with Netscape.

Take a second look at the horizontal rule dialog box that appears when you click on the HR icon from Hotdog (see fig. 3.10).

Fig. 3.10
You have lots of options for how your horizontal line appears.

- Width—You can choose a percentage or an absolute value for how long your line appears in your Netscape window. I recommend always using a percentage value.

- No Shading—Lets you decide if your horizontal line appears solid black or as a shaded line (the default setting).

- Alignment—Determines how the line is aligned on your screen. You can choose left, center, or right from the drop down menu bar. This feature is only useful when you specify the line width as well.

- Thickness—Sometimes you want a thicker line to separate your text. From the drop down box you can choose ten different thicknesses (2 is the default). It is extremely effective when you also select the No Shading box as well.

Figure 3.11 shows several different types of horizontal rule lines.

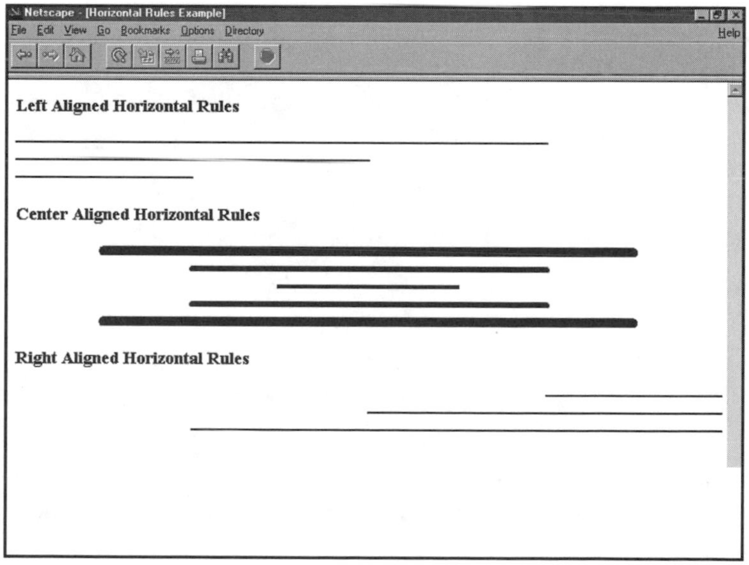

Fig. 3.11
Example of many different lines using Netscapes HR extensions.

Choose the specific options for your HR line and click on the **OK button**. Hotdog will create the HTML code for you automatically and insert a customized line for you.

Preformatted Text

Sometimes you don't want Netscape to take care of the formatting for you. You may want to type some information into your Hotdog and have it look exactly the same in Netscape, without worrying about paragraph tags.

In that case, use the <PRE> and </PRE> tags for preformatted text. Any text that appears within the <PRE> tags will appear exactly the same in Netscape, spaces, tabs, line breaks and all.

Add the preformatted tags into your Web page by clicking on the **Tags** button in Hotdog and choosing <PRE> from the available list of tags. See "Table Alternatives" in chapter 4 for more information (and an example) of using preformatted text on your home page.

Add Style to Your Text

The last section of this chapter deals with adding special formatting features to your text. Sometimes you might want to emphasize a specific word or italicize a phrase. Other times you may want to center a headline, or even make text stand out by having it blink intermittently.

Several text formatting features are available; some work with all browsers, and others only work with Netscape. Either way, these features can really add life to a home page.

Centering

Centering is probably my favorite text formatting feature. Using the center tags <CENTER> and </CENTER> you can make specific text and headlines stand out easily.

I like to use the center tags for my headlines, so they span the area where text appears, instead of being trapped on the left hand margin. To center text, highlight the area with your mouse and click on the **center icon** in Hotdog.

The center tags appear around the text you've highlighted. Try centering your main home page headline. After adding the tags, my HTML code now looks like this:

<CENTER><H1>Welcome to Andy's Home</H1></CENTER>

You can center headlines, horizontal lines, and paragraphs of text.

Bold Text

You can mark various words and phrases in your HTML document to be displayed in boldface using the <B> and </B> tags. Text surrounded by these tags appears darker and thicker then standard text, and stands out nicely on your home page.

Select text to be bolded and click on the **Bold** button in Hotdog.

The bold tags appear around that text.

> **Note**
>
> You can also mark text to be darker by using the <STRONG> and </STRONG> tags. The strong tags are a more general term that tell Netscape to make the marked text appear stronger on-screen. The strong tags are inherited from the parent language of HTML (SGML), but are not used as often now because each browser interpreted what strong text meant, creating some discrepancies. Everyone understands what bold means.

Italics

Marking some text to be italicized is just as easy, only you use the <I> and </I> tags instead. Hotdog makes it easy to mark italicized text by using the italics icon on the menu bar.

> **Note**
>
> Similar to the strong vs. bold debate outlined above, you can also emulate italics with other tags. The <EM> and </EM> tags, short for *emphasis* make marked text stand out typically by italicizing the text. The <EM> tags are used more often then the <STRONG> tags, but their use is dwindling.

Blinking

Arguably one of the most annoying features of Netscape–blinking text–is also able to be made to blink intermittently.

Judicious use of the <BLINK> and </BLINK> tags is accepted, but be careful not to make your home page look like a bad used car commercial.

To make text blink, highlight it with your mouse and click on the **Tags** button in Hotdog. Then choose blink from the list of available tags. See figure

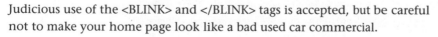

3.12 for a look at your HTML with these formatting tags added. Then look at figure 3.13 to see it in Netscape.

Fig. 3.12

An example of the text emphasis tags in HTML.

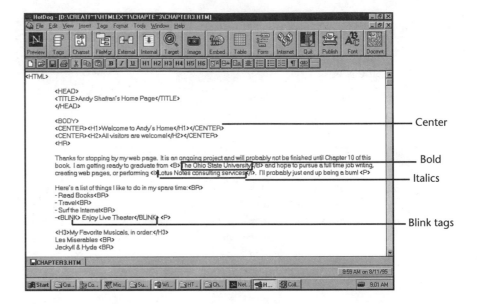

Center

Bold

Italics

Blink tags

Fig. 3.13

Here are the same tags in Netscape (of course, you can't see the blinking text).

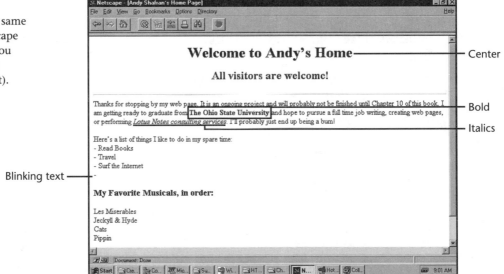

Center

Bold

Italics

Blinking text

Chapter 4

Adding Lists and Tables to Your Home Page

Most people like watching the nightly news because there is a lot of information packed into 30 minutes. The newscasters realize that they've got to keep the viewers' interest or the viewers will switch channels. Your home page needs to follow this same practice. You have to organize your page and present your information in a concise and senseful way, or they'll leave your page faster than clicking on the remote control.

With a simple home page underneath your belt, it's time to start exploring different HTML elements that can help you organize your page and present information more attractively.

This chapter teaches you how to add lists and tables to your home page. Lists and tables are HTML elements that make it easy to display groups of related information together in an easy-to-use format. You'll use lists to show itemized elements listed in order, while tables use a familiar row and column feel which allows you to display a lot of information in a concentrated area.

Although not difficult to use, lists and tables require a more thorough knowledge of Hotdog and HTML. Specifically, in this chapter I'll show you how to:

- Determine when to use a list on your home page
- Use three different kinds of lists
- Understand the differences between lists and tables
- Create a simple home page table
- Customize your table to make it look good

What are Lists and Tables?

Nowadays, lists are an integral part of virtually any home page. With several different types available, lists allow you to separate pieces of text and information away from the standard paragraph format. While a paragraph wraps text around line after line in a traditional format, lists show text differently. Items in a list are indented, separated from other paragraphs of text, and usually preceded with a bullet or number.

Proper use of a list makes a large amount of information readable, usable, and easy to spot on a home page. Additionally, lists can be embedded within each other to allow you to display data in outline format. Personally, I use lists on my home page to itemize my interests and organize my web page of hotlinks.

Related to lists, tables use a row and column format to place information on your home page. Supported only by Netscape and HTML 3.0 browsers, tables are relatively new to the WWW.

Tables are fantastic for displaying a lot of related information in a usable format that fits on your screen. Anything that you would organize in columns makes sense to use a table. Companies commonly use tables to show products and pricing information, and I use a table on my home page to compare and contrast Broadway musicals.

Both tables and lists offer specialized formatting options to let you customize how they appear on your home page.

What Lists Help You Accomplish

First off, I am going to show you what lists are and how you can use them in your home page. Lists are extremely popular and can make a good home page look great when used correctly.

I like to use lists in three major situations: when I have similar information that needs to be categorized in some fashion, when I have a lot of data that would be too wordy and unreadable in paragraph format, and when I have a step-by-step process that needs to be described in order.

Organize with Lists

Lists make it extremely easy to itemize information in a concise format. You don't have to bury important information inside of a long paragraph. Instead, use a list.

Take my home page as an example (http//www.cis.ohio-state.edu/~shafran). Originally, I had a paragraph that described my own personal interests:

> As a college student, I have a lot of time on my hands. Consequently, I have a varied group of interests. I work with a product called Lotus Notes which is groupware software (which I am interested in in general, as well). Besides Lotus Notes, I love browsing the WWW and seeing all the weird and useful pages. As a career, I write computer books about a wide variety of products. In my spare time I like to read and listen to (and see) Broadway musicals and live theater. <P>

Not only was the paragraph too wordy, but it presented a bunch of information repetitively and in an unorganized fashion. Figure 4.1 shows the same information in list format, and figure 4.2 is how Netscape displays it.

Fig. 4.1
Here's my personal interest list shown in Hotdog.

Fig. 4.2
Here's how my list
of information
appears in
Netscape.

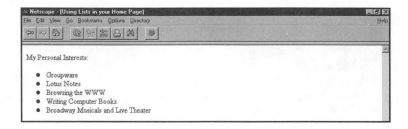

Lists help you get information organized and make people more likely to read through your home page, because they can scan through a list and find what they are looking for.

Simplify Large Amounts of Information

Whenever you have several items of related information, you should consider using a list to make it readable. For example, let's say I was creating a listing of my favorite Broadway musicals. Rather than typing the names of the musicals in paragraph form, creating a list is perfect for this situation.

Each musical is indented and easy to read (see fig. 4.3).

Fig. 4.3
Here are some of
my favorite musi-
cals. Which is
easier to read:
the paragraph
or the list?

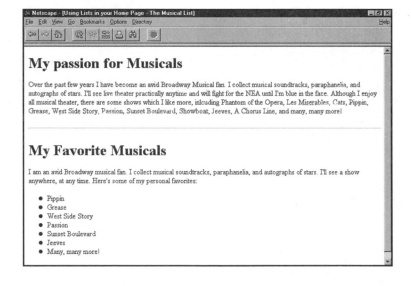

> **Note**
>
> In the last chapter I showed you how to use the <BR> tag to force Netscape to display text on the next line. Using the <BR> tag, you can emulate a simple list, although I usually wouldn't recommend it. Lists are indented, bulleted, and can even be numbered, making them much more powerful for displaying separate items than the <BR> tag.

Describe a Step by Step Process

Another popular use of lists within web pages is to describe a specific process one step at a time. HTML automatically numbers each step in ascending order, allowing you to ignore the actual numbering scheme for each step. These types of lists are perfect for creating a training manual.

Whenever you need to outline a process or describe a complicated series of events, I recommend using a list in your home page.

Add a List to Your Page

Now that you know when you can (and should) use lists, let's take a look at the different types of lists you can add to your home page. Check out figure 4.4 for a good example of when using a list makes sense.

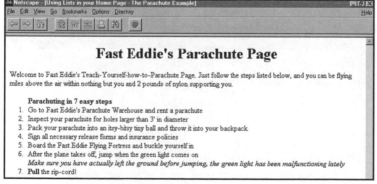

Fig. 4.4
Here's a step-by-step process that needs to be explicit about the order of operations

Lists come in three basic flavors: unordered, ordered, and definition. Although there are others, these are the most commonly used and most widely supported types. Each is similar in that it lists each item on subsequent lines and labels selected text to make information stand out. The main difference between these three list types is how the listed items are numbered and structured.

Adding a list to your home page is relatively easy. First you add the list opening and closing tags (<UL> and </UL>, <OL> and </OL>, or <DL> and </DL>). Then you add a separate tag before the text identifying each item in the list—the <LI> tag. Finally you add the title of the list inside of the header tags (<LH> and </LH>) and you're ready to go. Don't get too overwhelmed by all this HTML tagging. I'll step you through Hotdog to create them.

Tip

Notice the spaces after the <LI> tag and before the first letter in each element above. Make sure that you follow the same convention of always including a space between the <LI> tag or never including the space. Mixing and matching spaces between text and the <LI> tag will make your list look jumbled because Netscape displays spaces you type there. Be consistent, and all your items will line up correctly in your list.

Unordered (Bulleted) List

The most common list you will find on Web pages is the unordered list. Each item in an unordered list is identified by a miniature icon preceding it. With Netscape, you can display three different icons in front of your list items.

The HTML tags for the unordered list are <UL> and </UL>. Inside of those tags, you can specify each list item with the <LI> tag. To add an unordered list to your home page, click on **Insert**, **list** from the Hotdog menu bar to bring up the dialog box labeled **create list element,** shown in figure 4.5.

Tip

Although you can have as many list items as you want, be careful not to go overboard. A list with too many items is just as unattractive and unreadable as a large paragraph of text. As a general rule of thumb, I try to limit myself to no more than 8 items per list. Generally, if I need more items than that, I can divide my list into smaller sub-lists, which are easier to scan through.

Fig. 4.5
Hotdog makes it easy for you to add any type of list you want to your home page.

From here, you can choose which type of list you want to add and select your desired display options. Then, type your list's title in the **list heading** box. The list title appears above your list and serves as a label describing it. After that, choose the type of bulleted icon you want preceding each list item in the **type** box—circle, square, or disc. Only Netscape allows you to choose the type of icons you can display in unordered lists. Other browsers ignore this command and display their own set of icons automatically.

> **Note**
>
> My version of Netscape doesn't exactly display a square, circle, or disc when you use an unordered list. Instead, Netscape displays a filled square box, an unfilled square box, and circle, respectively.

The other options—**use image, use icon, compact list**, and **multi-column**—don't really affect how your list appears in Netscape. The first two options are HTML 3.0 based (which Netscape doesn't support—yet) and the second two are rarely used with unordered lists, if ever.

Click on the **OK** button and Hotdog inserts the necessary HTML code into your document. After the <LI> tag you can type the information you want to appear for that list item. For subsequent list items, type in the text, highlight it, and click on the unordered list icon. Hotdog inserts the <LI> tag for you automatically. Eventually, your list will look like figures 4.6 and 4.7:

II

Creating Web Pages

Fig. 4.6

Here's my listing for Barney's Circus Animals in Hotdog.

Fig. 4.7

Here's how my list looks when using Netscape to view it.

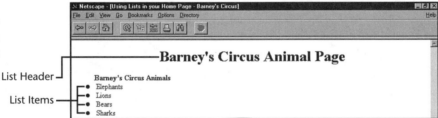

Ordered (Numbered) List

Similar to an unordered list, the ordered list works in much the same way. The only difference between the two list types is that instead of inserting graphical bullets in front of items of information, the ordered list adds sequential numbers or letters in front of your list items automatically. This saves you from manually typing a number for each item in the list. It is a real help when you insert an item at tip top of list— Netscape renumbers for you automatically.

The ordered list uses the <OL> and </OL> tags. Just like the unordered list, you also use the <LI> to identify each element. By default, ordered lists number each element, beginning with one.

I use ordered lists to describe information that I want ranked in order (think of Letterman's Top 10 List—he uses an ordered list), or to describe each step in a process that must be followed in order.

Adding an ordered list to your home page with Hotdog is just as easy as adding an unordered one. Choose **Insert**, **list** from the menu bar. Then choose **numbered** from the list type box.

In the drop down **Type** box, choose the way in which you want to label each of your list elements. The default is numerical values (1, 2, 3, . . .). You can choose between numbers, letters, and Roman numerals. Once you've chosen how to number your list items, you can pick which number to begin with. The default is 1. Type in a number in the **First Number** box to create a list beginning with a different value. Click on the **OK** button to create the HTML required.

Just like the unordered list, you can add as many <LI> elements as you want to your list of items; but remember not to go overboard. Figure 4.8 shows a simple unordered list in Hotdog and figure 4.9 shows it in Netscape after clicking the preview button.

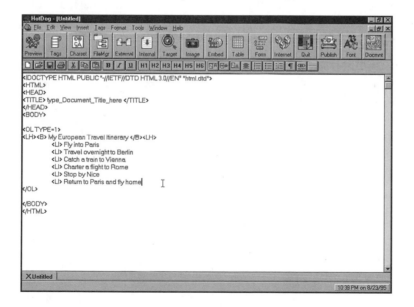

Fig. 4.8
Here's my listing for my travel itinerary.

Fig. 4.9
The Netscape view
of my European
trip itinerary, in
order of my visits.

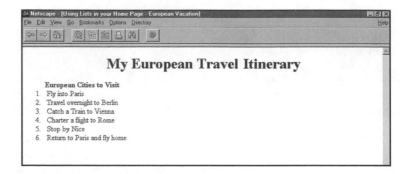

Tip

Use the ordered list icon from the Hotdog menu bar to easily mark text as additional
items in your list.

Definition List

While definition lists are not as common as ordered and unordered lists, they
can come in handy in several situations. Using two lines instead of one for
each list item, the definition list is useful when you want to add additional
information to your list elements.

Definition lists work slightly differently than other types of lists. Instead of
having a single <LI> tag for each element, the definition list requires two tags.
The <DT> tag is used to identify text listed as a separate element, commonly
known as the *term being defined*. The <DD> tag places the following information indented and below the <DT> text. That information is referred to as the
definition. One look at a definition list and you'll immediately understand
where it gets its name.

Add a definition list just like the other two lists, except choose **definition
list** in the create list element dialog box.

Of course, a dictionary is the ideal use for a definition list. You can list each
term and its definition easily in HTML. However, you'll soon find many other
users for a definition list in your home page.

Instead of using an unordered list to show my favorite Broadway musicals,
here's how I use a definition list (see fig. 4.10). Look at figure 4.11 to see how
Netscape displays my definition list.

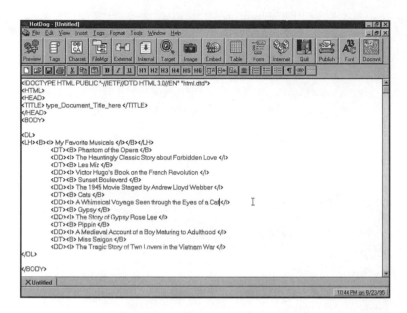

Fig. 4.10
Here's my listing of favorite Broadway musicals.

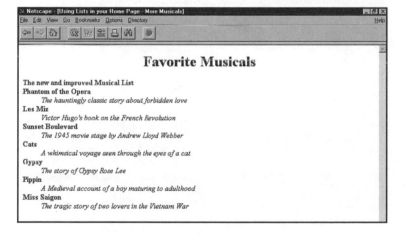

Fig. 4.11
My musical list now has a little more style to it.

Lists within Lists

One nice feature of lists is the ability to recursively place them inside each other. Creating lists within lists allows you to have several levels of organized material. You can embed several levels of lists on your home page.

Adding a list within a list is the same process as creating a single list. There are no special HTML tags—just the regular list tags. Make sure you use the closing tag for each sub-list </UL>, otherwise Netscape may get confused. You can even embed different types of lists within each other.

> **Tip**
>
> When you add lists inside of lists, make sure you line up each level of the list with tabs when you are creating your home page. Although the tabs won't show up under Netscape, lists are much easier to maintain and read if they are organized well.

Here's an example of adding several sub-lists within a larger one (see figs. 4.12 and 4.13):

Fig. 4.12
Here's how Hotdog shows a bunch of lists bundled into a large one.

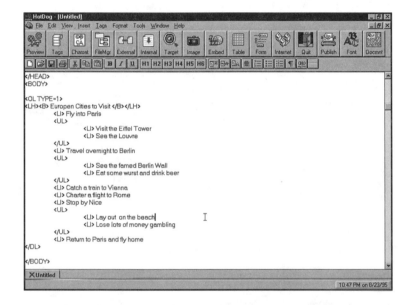

Fig. 4.13
My European itinerary is starting to get in shape.

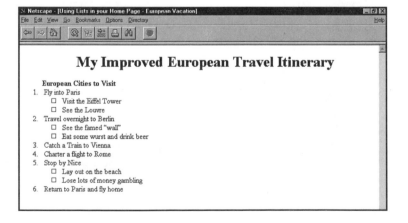

Tabling Your Home Page

The one drawback of using lists is that they are one-dimensional objects. This means that you can only organize information on subsequent lines. Tables, on the other hand, allow you to line up data in organized rows and columns. You get the flexibility of having two dimensions to display information on your home page.

It's important to understand appropriate times to use tables, so they don't waste space on your web page. I tend to use tables to compare and contrast similar pieces of information because you can use several different columns and rows. Each row and column can be labeled, allowing you to emulate a spreadsheet-type appearance.

A good table can make your home page look very neat and organized and offer a lot of information to the viewer at the same time. A bad, or inappropriate, table splits up your page and makes the point you are trying to convey confusing. Figure 4.14 shows a sample table.

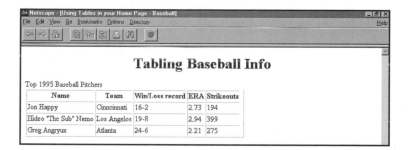

Fig. 4.14
Here's a table that may come in handy to baseball fans.

Caution

Tables are one of the biggest Netscape-only features that I talk about in this book. Be aware that anyone who uses another browser will see a bunch of jumbled text. Figure 4.15 shows the same table, only viewed with a non-table-supporting browser (Mosaic 1.0).

Since virtually everyone uses Netscape, and new browsers are supporting tables, I wouldn't lose too much sleep over this, but you should be aware of this issue.

II

Creating Web Pages

Fig. 4.15
Don't worry—
Mosaic 2.0 and
other browsers are
now beginning to
support tables.

Add a Table

Adding tables to your home page can be complicated because several different tags are used. There is a <TABLE> and </TABLE> that surround the entire table, and several other tags that define how information should appear. See table 4.1 for a complete description of table tags.

Table 4.1 HTML Tags	
Tag	**Description**
<TABLE> and </TABLE>	Surrounds the entire table. This tag tells Netscape to expect the other table tags listed below. Add the word BORDER (<TABLE BORDER> and </TABLE>) to this tag if you want a grid to appear, separating each row and column with a thin line.
<CAPTION> and </CAPTION>	Text within these tags serves as the tables explanatory caption. You use <TC> and </TC> as well.
<TH> and </TH>	Slightly enlarges and bold text to serve as row and column headers.
<TR> and </TR>	Identifies each row in the table. The </TR> isn't critical, but makes your HTML code more complete.
<TD> and </TD>	The text that should go into each cell in the table is surrounded by these tags.

Adding all those tags up makes it confusing to create a multi-row table if you're not careful. Remember that simple table for baseball fans? Figure 4.16 shows the HTML that was used to create it. You can't see it all because it's so long.

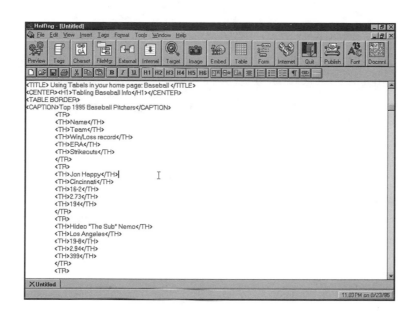

Fig. 4.16
There's a lot of
HTML for even a
small table.

Whew, all that just for a little table, and I spent extra time formatting the
HTML into an easy to read format by adding tabs to line up each element.
Fortunately for us, a nice automatic table creator is built into Hotdog. Once
you get the hang of using Hotdog, you'll be able to add new tables easily.
You'll also learn the HTML specifics so you can modify and create great look-
ing tables.

Follow these steps to add a simple table to your home page:

1. Click on the icon labeled **Table** to bring up the create table dialog box
   (see fig. 4.17).

Fig. 4.17
Here's my table,
all ready to be
created.

2. To create the same table above, type **Top 1995 Baseball Pitchers**. You can choose to display the caption above or below the table. Unless your table is exceedingly small, leave the caption above it so viewers can look at the caption first.

3. In the **columns** and **rows** boxes, type in the number of each you would like in your table. Rows and columns that you want to use as labels should be included in this count. I'm going to put **4** in the **rows** box and **5** in the **columns** box for my table. Hotdog creates the table for you in the box labeled **sample table**.

4. Type how many heading columns and/or rows you want to have in the **heading cols** and **heading rows** boxes. Hotdog shades in the heading boxes in the **sample table** box to make them easy to identify. I only want a single heading row, so I type **1** in that box and leave the other one blank.

5. Select how thick of a border you want for your table. I like a simple border so I am going to put a 1 in the **border width** box.

> **Note**
>
> Here's a rundown of the other boxes in the create table dialog box: width and height let you set the table's dimensions; cell padding and cell spacing let you add spaces between your tables, rows, and columns; and alignment buttons allow you to set where in each cell your text is aligned (left, right, or centered).

6. Now type your information in each box listed in the **sample table**. The shaded gray boxes are the table headers and the white boxes represent each table cell. Use your mouse, arrow, and tab keys to maneuver around the **sample table**.

7. When you're finished, click on the **OK** button and Hotdog creates all the HTML code for you (see fig. 4.18).

Fig. 4.18
Yech, look at that jumbled mess of tags and text.

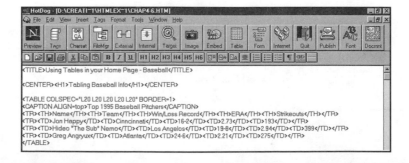

Tip

It's a good idea to take some time and format your table tags and text to be easily read, in case you want to make changes later. Trying to update the text shown in figure 4.18 is much simpler when it is naturally readable. I spaced my table out to make it readable using tabs and carriage returns.

Using Advanced Table Features

Now that you can create a good-looking, simple table, let's try adding a little flavor to it. Netscape offers several impressive ways of customizing your tables.

I'm not going to go into excruciating detail for each of these options because you have to type them in yourself (Hotdog doesn't support them—yet), and they can be overwhelming. I'll explain each one and give you an example of how they can help you organize your home page tables.

Lines Spanning Multiple Rows

As you start using tables more and more often, you'll occasionally find situations where you wish your information could span multiple rows. That's where the ROWSPAN tag comes into use.

ROWSPAN is a special keyword that you add to the <TD> tag for a specific cell. To have a cell span two columns instead of the default 1, instead of using `<TD>Your Cells Text Here</TD>`, try this instead:

<TD ROWSPAN=2>Your extended Text HERE</TD>

When your table displays, you'll now be taking up two rows for the cell you added ROWSPAN to. Here's how I used ROWSPAN to change my baseball table:

```
<TR>

<TD>Jon Happy</TD>

<TD ROWSPAN=2>Cincinnati</TD>

<TD>16-2</TD>

<TD>2.73</TD>

<TD>194</TD>

</TR>
```

```
<TR>

<TD>Jose Rio</TD>

<TD>28-2</TD>

<TD>1.92</TD>

<TD>199</TD>

</TR>
```

Figure 4.19 shows the changed table in Netscape.

Fig. 4.19
Here's how
ROWSPAN could
shape up your
table.

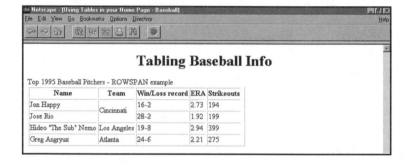

> **Caution**
>
> When you use ROWSPAN (or COLSPAN, described next), make sure you take into account the reduced number of rows or columns you need to fill for other table entries. For example, I had one less column of information for Jose Rio above when I entered his row (<TR> </TR>) of information.

Spanning Multiple Columns

As in ROWSPAN, you can also have specific cells span multiple columns as well. Using the built-in keyword COLSPAN, you can instruct your table to span across as many cells as you wish.

Use COLSPAN just like you did ROWSPAN:

```
<TR>

<TH COLSPAN=2>Personal Information</TH>

<TH COLSPAN=3>Statistics</TH>

</TR>
```

```
<TR>

<TH>Name</TH>

<TH>Team</TH>

<TH>Win/Loss record</TH>

<TH>ERA</TH>

<TH>Strikeouts<TH>

</TR>
```

Look at figure 4.20 to see my COLSPAN in action.

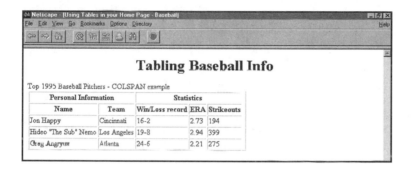

Fig. 4.20
You can use ROWSPAN and COLSPAN in the <TH> tags as well.

Embedding Lists into Tables

Tables can be treated just like any other HTML element and be broken down into lists as described earlier in this chapter. All three list types perform the same when embedded within a table. Make sure you carefully add the closing tags when you add a list to your table—they are easy to lose track of.

In figure 4.21, I've added a simple unordered list to my baseball table.

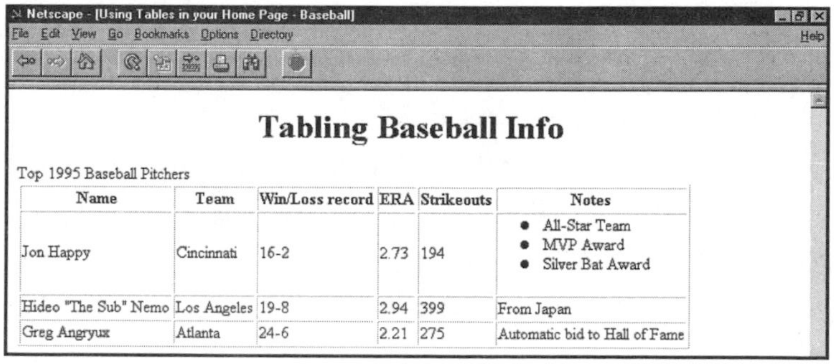

Fig. 4.21
Lists inside of tables look really slick—don't you agree?

> **Note**
>
> If you really are looking for a challenge, try embedding a table within a table. The effects are neat, but keeping track of your HTML can be a bear! You've got to make sure you use all of the closing tags properly (</TABLE>), and lining up each element is difficult. Embedded tables often don't need a header or a border.

Setting Your Text Alignment

Netscape tables also let you customize the alignment of each cell, both vertically and horizontally. Also set by special keywords, ALIGN and VALIGN, these alignment settings offer you increased flexibility in how your table should look. Hotdog lets you set your table alignment in the create table dialog box (but not your vertical alignment setting).

The ALIGN and VALIGN keywords can each have three settings and are used in the same spot as the spanning keywords above—within the <TD> tag. Use table 4.2 to understand the use of these two keywords:

Table 4.2   Keyword Setting Descriptions

Keyword Setting	Description
ALIGN=LEFT	Left justifies text in the cell
ALIGN=CENTER	Centers the text horizontally within the cell
ALIGN=RIGHT	Right justifies text in the cell
VALIGN=TOP	Aligns text to the top of the cell (particularly useful when an element in the row has multiple lines of information)
VALIGN=MIDDLE	The default setting, centers text vertically in the cell
VALIGN=BOTTOM	Lines text up with the bottom of the cell.

In the previous example, I added the VALIGN=TOP to the entire row that had the list within it so that my text doesn't appear floating in the middle of the cell. I change my <TABLE> tag to:

<TABLE VALIGN=TOP>

Now my baseball table looks like figure 4.22.

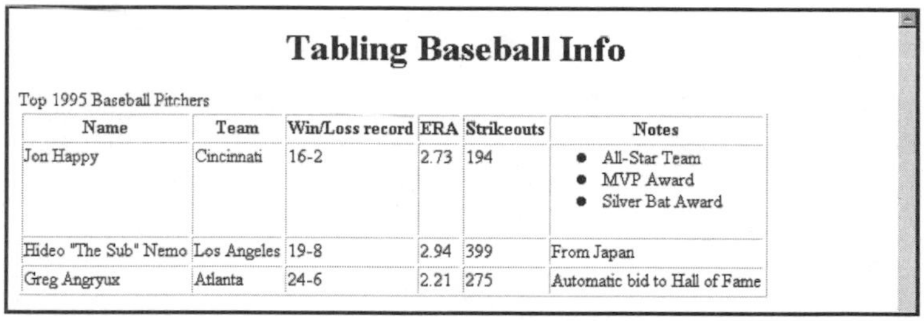

Fig. 4.22
My baseball pitchers' information is now lined to the top of the cell.

Tip

Several Web pages use the ALIGN and VALIGN to organize graphics within a table. By removing the table's border, you can perfectly line up sets of graphics in an organized fashion.

Table Alternatives

If you are concerned that non-Netscape browsers can't display tables, find them to bulky to use, or would prefer to not use them at all, you'll be pleased to find that there are a few popular options to using tables.

The two most popular options are using extra lists, or the <PRE> and </PRE> HTML tags. These two workarounds offer table-like functionality but are limited in nature.

Lists Can Replace Tables

Even though lists are one dimensional displays of information, if properly used, you can replace virtually any table with a couple of lists.

Take the baseball player table that I've been using. I could replace that table with afew lists (see fig. 4.23). Of course it's not as easy to read as a table, and makes the user scroll through the screen.

Preformatted Text

In chapter 3, I talked about the <PRE> and </PRE> tags which display information as you actually type it on your home page, without any Netscape interpretations on how it should be presented.

Fig. 4.23
Although they
present the same
amount of
information, lists
aren't as flexible as
tables.

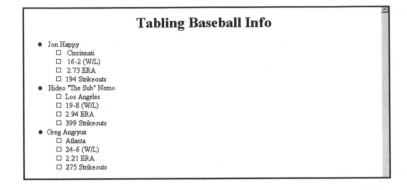

You can use these tags to emulate a table as well. It's not as flashy, and you can't have graphical borders, but most people won't even notice the difference. Using carriage returns, spaces, and tabs, I've created the same table as preformatted text (see fig. 4.24).

```
<PRE><B>

Name                        Team                    (W/L)
ERA                         Strikeouts</B>

Jon Happy                   Cincinnati         ·    16-2
2.73                        194

Hideo "The Sub" Nemo        Los Angeles             19-8
2.94                        399

Greg Angryux                Atlanta                 24-6
2.21                        275

</PRE>
```

Fig. 4.24
The <PRE> tag lets
me replace this
simple table with
no problems.

Tabling Baseball Info				
Name	**Team**	**(W/L)**	**ERA**	**Strikeouts**
Jon Happy	Cincinnati	16-2	2.73	194
Hideo "The Sub" Nemo	Los Angeles	19-8	2.94	399
Greg Angryux	Atlanta	24-6	2.21	275

Tip

You can even use text formatting tags within your pre-formatted text to bold or italicize different parts of your table.

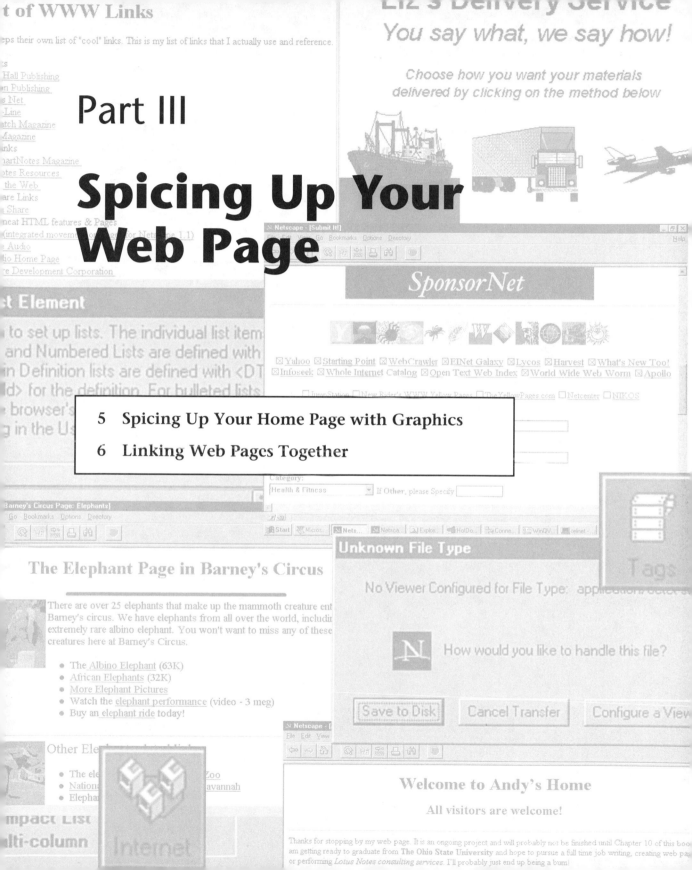

Part III

Spicing Up Your Web Page

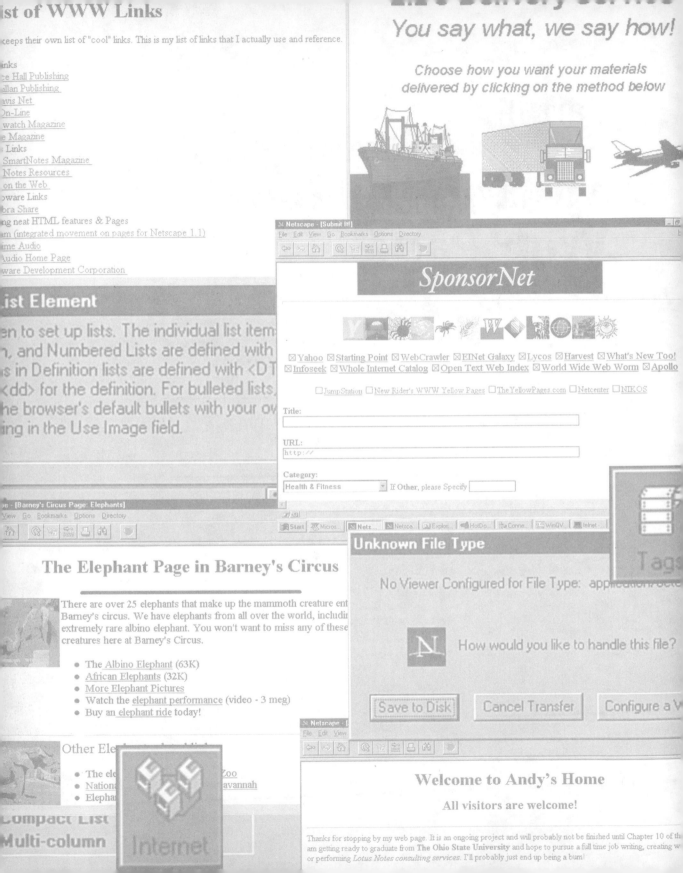

ist of WWW Links

...keeps their own list of "cool" links. This is my list of links that I actually use and reference.

inks
...ce Hall Publishing
...llan Publishing
...avis Net
...On-Line
...watch Magazine
...e Magazine
... Links
...SmartNotes Magazine
...Notes Resources
... on the Web
...ware Links
...bra Share
...ng neat HTML features & Pages
...um (integrated movement on pages for Netscape 1.1)
...me Audio
...Audio Home Page
...ware Development Corporation

ist Element

...en to set up lists. The individual list item...
..., and Numbered Lists are defined with...
...s in Definition lists are defined with <DT...
...<dd> for the definition. For bulleted lists,...
...he browser's default bullets with your ov...
...ing in the Use Image field.

You say what, we say how!

Choose how you want your materials
delivered by clicking on the method below

Netscape - [Submit It!]
File Edit View Go Bookmarks Options Directory

SponsorNet

☒ Yahoo ☒ Starting Point ☒ WebCrawler ☒ EINet Galaxy ☒ Lycos ☒ Harvest ☒ What's New Too!
☒ Infoseek ☒ Whole Internet Catalog ☒ Open Text Web Index ☒ World Wide Web Worm ☒ Apollo

☐ JumpStation ☐ New Rider's WWW Yellow Pages ☐ TheYellowPages.com ☐ Netcenter ☐ NIKOS

Title:

URL:
http://

Category:
Health & Fitness   ▼ If Other, please Specify

...Start Micros... Nets... Netsca Explor... HotDo... Conne... WinQV... Telnet...

Unknown File Type

No Viewer Configured for File Type: application/oc...

How would you like to handle this file?

Save to Disk   Cancel Transfer   Configure a V...

e - [Barney's Circus Page: Elephants]
View Go Bookmarks Options Directory

The Elephant Page in Barney's Circus

There are over 25 elephants that make up the mammoth creature ent...
Barney's circus. We have elephants from all over the world, includir...
extremely rare albino elephant. You won't want to miss any of these...
creatures here at Barney's Circus.

- The Albino Elephant (63K)
- African Elephants (32K)
- More Elephant Pictures
- Watch the elephant performance (video - 3 meg)
- Buy an elephant ride today!

Other Ele...

- The ele...   Zoo
- Nationa...   avannah
- Elepha...

Compact List

Multi-column

Internet

Netscape - ...
File Edit View

Welcome to Andy's Home

All visitors are welcome!

Thanks for stopping by my web page. It is an ongoing project and will probably not be finished until Chapter 10 of th...
am getting ready to graduate from **The Ohio State University** and hope to pursue a full time job writing, creating w...
or performing *Lotus Notes consulting services*. I'll probably just end up being a bum!

Chapter 5

Spicing Up Your Home Page with Graphics

You're already halfway through this book, and you've got a decent looking home page to prove it. So far, I've shown you how to plan and produce a good looking home page that isn't too complicated to update and take care of.

Now that you're familiar with lists, tables and text formatting features, you can organize your page however you like. But text formatting isn't the real reason the WWW is so popular, it's the ability to add cool graphics and pictures to your page alongside your text.

As you've probably already noticed, almost every page on the WWW uses graphics or pictures to enhance their site and make it more enjoyable to visit. This chapter teaches you how to spice up your home page with vivid graphics, colorful backgrounds, and useful icons. You probably won't even recognize your own home page when you're finished with this chapter!

In this chapter, you learn how to:

- Use the images included on the home page CD
- Add images to your home page
- Customize your home page with icons
- Change your page's background to a specific color or pattern

Pros and Cons of Web Page Graphics

You've probably spent a lot of time browsing through many different sites on the Web. You've seen personal pages, commercial pages, and lots of other unique Web sites, and I'll bet that almost every one of them used images in some fashion. Everything from business logos and snazzy icons to pet pictures and famous paintings can be found on the WWW. Remember the Coca-Cola example?

Images and graphics are vital to the Web's existence. The WWW is the only Internet tool that lets you look at images and text on the same screen at the same time. Imagine picking up an issue of *Newsweek* that had no pictures in it. It would probably be pretty boring, no matter *how* they formatted their text. Looking at a Web page without any graphics is like reading a coffee table book that has no pictures. It just doesn't make much sense.

You'll learn how you can easily add images and pictures to your home page to make it more attractive and fun to browse. See figure 5.1 for a prime example of a Web site that takes advantage of graphics.

Fig. 5.1

Can you just imagine the Louvre (**http://www.emf.net/wm/paint/auth/michelangelo/**) Web site without pictures?

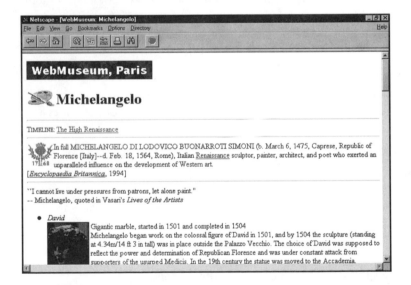

Of course there are exceptions to the rule of using images on your Web page, but they are few and far between. For example, the Yahoo WWW index (see fig. 5.2) is arguably one of the most useful sites on the entire Web, but you won't find an image in the entire site.

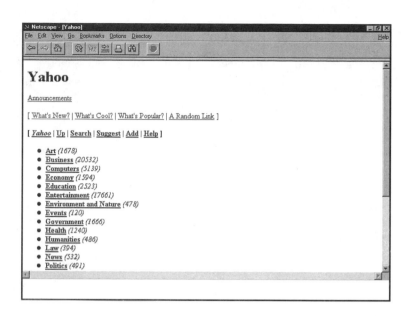

Fig. 5.2
Yahoo (**http://
www.yahoo.com**)
is one of the most
used and best
known spots on
the WWW.

Generally though, if you aren't taking advantage of the WWW's ability to
display images, your pages are probably pretty boring.

On the flip side, you've also got to be careful not to overdo your home page
with too many images. Before you read this chapter and decide to add 100+
images to your one Web page, remember that it's easy to go overboard. With
too many icons and images lining your home page, your text will get lost in
the shuffle, visitors won't understand what they're looking at, and all your
efforts for a great looking home page could be for naught.

The best solution is to balance your use of graphics in your home page. If
you're not sure whether your home page is too plain or too busy, ask a friend
for their opinion, but remember that ultimately your home page reflects you
and your personality.

Where You Can Find Graphics, Images, and Pictures

Now that you're convinced that you need to add an image or two to your
home page, where do you find them? Acquiring images can be the most difficult task in the entire process. Whether you want a simple icon or a pan-
oramic view of the Grand Canyon, it's hard to find that perfect image to stick
in your home page.

III

Spicing It Up!

Realizing this, I've included hundreds of different images, icons, and backgrounds on the CD-ROM in the back of this book. You have animals, famous people, neat icons, and radiant backgrounds directly at your fingertips. And if these don't fit your needs, I've also included some tips on how you can get your own images into your home page.

On the Enclosed CD-ROM

When we were putting together the enclosed CD-ROM, we asked ourselves this question: What kind of stuff would people find useful on a CD-ROM in this book? The first answer that jumped to my mind was graphics. I'm talking about images, icons, pictures, drawings, sketches, and lots more! This CD is your main resource when creating your own home page, and I've included all the appropriate material.

I've organized the images on the CD-ROM into three main categories:

- Pictures—You can find shots of animals, famous people, and lots of other images that should look familiar. This is a generic set of pictures that you may be able to use in your home page.

- Icons—Icons are used to represent information in a familiar and graphical way. On the CD you can find construction icons, home icons, navigation icons, even spiffy looking lines that can replace the <HR> tag!

- Backgrounds—Covered later this chapter, Netscape allows you to place an image behind your text so it appears as a background. This image gives your home page some flair and makes it much more colorful. Several hundred sample backgrounds are on the CD so you have plenty of choices.

Create Your Own

While you'll probably find lots of useful and nice images on the CD-ROM, you're also likely to want to put a few of your own customized pictures on your home page. You may want to show yourself, your family, or even a pet. I have pictures of myself and my family interspersed on my page.

To put your images on your home page, you'll need to scan them directly into your computer. Scanning is the process of digitizing an existing picture so it can be displayed on your PC. You can scan photographs, drawings, and logos directly into your computer to be added to your home page easily.

Unfortunately, the only way to scan pictures is with a separate piece of computer equipment called a scanner. Scanners range in price from $79 (black and white) to $999 (high-end color scanner) and are sold in most computer stores. If you intend to put a lot of images on your home page, purchasing a scanner may be a worthwhile investment.

> ### Tip
>
> For my home page, I didn't buy a scanner. Instead, I went down to my local copying store and rented their high-quality scanner for an hour or two. I paid about $25 and I got everything scanned and taken care of in one step. Figure 5.3 shows you one of the pictures that I scanned.

Fig. 5.3
Here's my brother in a photograph that I scanned myself. The resolution of the image looks fine.

Borrow from Other Pages

Another common way of obtaining images for your home page is to borrow them from other pages that you've visited. Built into Netscape, you can automatically save any image you see into a separate file with just a few mouse clicks.

Here's how to save an image that you're looking at in Netscape for Windows.

1. I'm going to show you how to borrow an image form my home page (I'm sure you don't care for a picture of me, but this same procedure works on any and every Web site you visit). Go to **http://www.cis.ohio-state.edu/~shafran**. When viewing a page, move your cursor over the image you want to save separately on your computer.

III

Spicing It Up!

   2. Click the right mouse button on the picture of me (and my sweetheart)
       at the top of the screen to bring up several Netscape options (see
       fig. 5.4).

Fig. 5.4
Netscape doesn't
support copyright
laws very well,
does it?

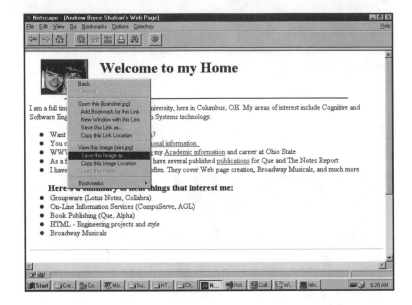

   3. Choose **Save this image as...** from the list of options to bring up a
       Save As dialog box as shown in figure 5.5.

Fig. 5.5
Once you click on
Save, the image is
yours forever.

   4. Netscape fills in the default file name automatically. Choose where on
       your hard drive you want to save the image and then click on the **Save**
       button.

Caution

Be aware that many images you might see when browsing on the WWW are protected under copyright laws. Even though you can save images with Netscape, you must have permission to use borrowed images on your own home page. You have permission to use all the images found on the home page CD included in this book.

Adding an Image to Your Home Page

Now that you know where to get images from, let's start adding them to your home page. This section uses Hotdog to add images to your home page and teaches you how to use the various HTML options when adding images.

I will explain what you need to understand about images and their file types. Then I'll describe how to add a simple image to your home page. I'm also going to give some image tips and tricks that will make your home page easier to use and more enjoyable for visitors who stop by.

Using the Proper Image File Types

There are several different formats that images can be saved in. These formats each have their own advantages and disadvantages for usage. On the WWW, two main image formats are most commonly supported: GIF and JPEG.

The GIF (Graphical Interchange Format) file type was pioneered by CompuServe (the Information Service) to provide information in a standard graphical format. GIF set an image standard years ago and was the first file type supported by the WWW.

Recently, a newer image format, labeled JPEG (Joint Photographic Experts Group) was developed and has proven to be significantly more efficient than GIFs in several circumstances, especially larger images. This means that JPEG files tend to be smaller and consequently download quicker when browsing the WWW. JPEG uses a special image compression technique that makes it better for pictures and snapshots. It handles colors and detail better than the GIF format.

Netscape supports both GIF and JPEG file types. Personally, I use JPEG for most of my images because of the significant file size difference, but in this book I'll talk about using both types of images. Not all browsers support JPEG (most of the newer ones do).

For your convenience, I've included a program on the CD-ROM so you can switch images from one format to another easily. Use Paint Shop Pro to convert any images between various graphics formats such as GIF to JPEG or vice versa.

> ### Tip
>
> Netscape allows you to use other image formats (such as PCX, TIF, and BMP), only you need a separate image viewer to see pictures in these formats. Check the CD-ROM out for additional image viewers.

Adding the Image

This example should look familiar to you. I'm using Barney's Circus home page to show you how adding graphics can make quite a difference. We'll build a special page for the human-eating tigers! See figure 5.6 for a plain text-only page.

Fig. 5.6
Here's the initial boring tiger page.

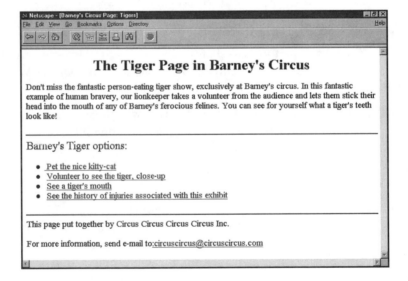

Adding images with Hotdog is pretty easy. Simply put your cursor at the spot you want to place the image and **click** on the **image icon** to bring up the insert image dialog box shown in figure 5.7. For my tiger page, I'm going to add the image to the top of my page, right above my <H1> </H1> header. You can place images anywhere on your home page between the <BODY and </BODY> tags.

Select a previously inserted image

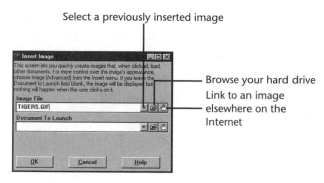

Browse your hard drive
Link to an image
elsewhere on the
Internet

Fig. 5.7
Type the image's
file name that you
want to add to
your home page.

Images are defined in HTML with the <IMG SRC=> tag. So to insert a GIF file named **TIGERS.GIF** into your home page, Hotdog adds the following line of HTML:

<IMG SRC=TIGERS.GIF>

That tag tells Netscape to display an image whose source filename is **TIGERS.GIF**. When you view your home page, the image will appear integrated along with your text.

Type the full file and path name of the image in the **image file** box. On the right of the box are three icons (explained in table 5.1) that may help you create the path and file name of your image.

Table 5.1   Image File Icon Table

To...	Do This...
Select a previously inserted image	Hotdog keeps track of the last few images you've added to your home page.
Click images	Click the icon to bring up a list of images inserted recently.
Browse your hard drive	Built into Hotdog is a mini file manager. Click on this icon to browse through the files on your hard drive and add images to your home page by selecting them.
Link to an image elsewhere on the Internet	You can also link directly to an image at a different spot on the WWW. Clicking on this button brings up a separate dialog box where you can build the URL. I talk more about linking it in the next chapter.

III

Spicing It Up!

Use the icons or type in your image's filename yourself. I'll type in TIGERS.GIF to add a feline picture to my tiger page; click on the **OK** button to add the proper HTML tags to your home page.

Images are defined in HTML with the <IMG SRC=> tag. To insert a GIF file named **TIGERS.GIF** into your home page, you would add the following line of HTML:

<IMG SRC=TIGERS.GIF>

That tag tells Netscape to display an image whose source file name is **TIGERS.GIF**. When you view your home page, the image will appear integrated along with your text.

Figure 5.8 shows the same page above, with the TIGERS.GIF image added to it.

Fig. 5.8
Just one image makes a page instantly more attractive!

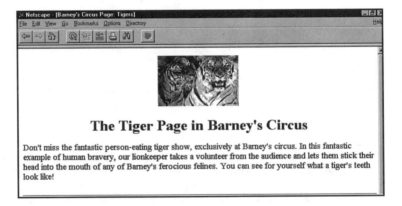

Note

Linking Netscape correctly to your images requires that you understand how to point to files that are in a different file directory or even on a different drive.

For example, if your image (TIGERS.GIF) is located in the exact same directory as the HTML file, you don't have to worry about pointing to other directories and drives. Your HTML tag is:

```
<IMG SRC=TIGERS.GIF>
```

But eventually, your home page images and HTML text may not be located in the same directory. If your images are located in a separate sub-directory named **IMAGES**, then your tag would be:

```
<IMG SRC=IMAGES/TIGERS.GIF>
```

If your images are located in a directory one level above your current sub-directory in your hard drive structure, then you would use this tag:

```
<IMG SRC=../TIGERS.GIF>
```

And if your image is located on a separate drive—like your D: drive— then you would use this tag, telling Netscape to look for the correct file:

```
<IMG SRC=FILE:///D:\TIGERS.GIF>
```

Any combination of the above tags can be used to tell Netscape where to look for your images when trying to display your home page.

Image File Size Guidelines

One of the most important things you should think about when it comes to using images in your home page is the file size. Whenever someone visits your home page, they must download all the text and images to their personal computer. Although text doesn't take very long to download, images can take awhile, so you want to be aware of how large your home page is and how long it takes to download.

Think of when you have to call a company on the phone for support and you have to push different buttons on your phone to get sent to the correct extension. After that, you usually have to wait until a support representative becomes available. You're on the phone just waiting, when you could probably be doing other things you enjoy more (like anything). If you hang up and call again later, you've still got to go through the same rigmarole.

This example is similar to what happens when people stop by your home page. Your home page immediately starts appearing, but they have to wait until all the text and images are loaded before they can continue. They've got to watch their computer download each image one at a time. Of course, the longer they wait, the more impatient they become.

Since waiting around is something that is almost universally annoying, I'll give you a few pointers on how you can make sure that visitors don't have to go get a cup of coffee every time they stop by your home page (after one or two visits, they may not come back again).

Maximum File Size

As a general rule of thumb, I try to limit any image on my home page to 20K. With a 20K limit, your images can be of sufficient detail, yet not make visitors chew off their fingernails waiting for the page to download. Actually, I use 20K as a very rough guideline. In the next section when I talk about icons, you'll find that most of them are extremely small (2-6K) and download quickly. Occasionally, you might have a fantastic image that is larger than 20K. Don't worry too much about using it; just be aware that if you add too many larger images, they add up quickly.

> **Tip**
>
> It's also a good idea to keep track of your entire home page's file size. Add up the size of your HTML file and the file size of each image you use. Your total should rest below 150K, preferably between 30-70K. With a 14.4 baud modem, visitors who stop by will spend 1-2 minutes downloading 150K before they can enjoy the full glory of your page. That's a long time to wait.

Resizing and Thumbnailing Your Images

If all the images you like are larger, you have several other options for including them on your home page without making each visitor download them. You can resize most of your images, making them smaller on-screen, and decreasing their actual file size as well.

Several professional packages, such as Adobe Photoshop, allow you to manipulate image sizes. Included on the home page CD, you'll find several Shareware tools that will let you resize your images. Although not nearly as robust as Photoshop, they're much cheaper (free) and can accomplish most of what you need for your home page. I use Paint Shop Pro or WinJPG to resize and create thumbnails of all my graphics. For simple tasks, they're nearly as good as commercial graphics packages.

Resizing makes your image smaller, and sometimes harder to see. Some images look fine when shrunk, others become barely readable. I've had great success resizing my images. One image I use was originally the size of the entire screen and took up 190K (what a long download for that single image). After resizing it to about one-fourth the screen size, the picture is down to about 43K, a reasonable size for my home page (although still large).

Another option, related to resizing your images, is creating thumbnail images. Thumbnail images are miniature duplicates of larger images. You could create a small thumbnail of a large image on your home page, and include a link to the full-size image that visitors can see if they wish. (Read "Linking Your Images" in chapter 6 for more information on how to do this.)

Thumbnails are extremely popular because they let visitors pick and choose which full size images they want from a cornucopia of miniature ones. See figure 5.9 for an example of how I use thumbnailed images in my home page.

Thumbnail size   Full Size image

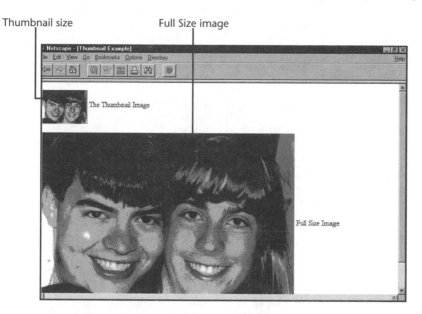

Fig. 5.9
The thumbnail image is at the top of my home page. Clicking on it brings up the same image full size.

Tip

If your images are all in GIF format, try converting them into JPEG format. You might notice a four to one file size difference from GIF to JPEG for certain images!

Manipulating Your Home Page Images

With images added, you'll notice a big difference on the attractiveness and appearance of your home page. However, there are several other HTML options which will help you manipulate and organize images. One of the most important of these lets you provide alternative text for visitors to read if they can't view your images for any reason.

Several of these HTML options will only work with Netscape—and they're worth using. You can set image alignment, text flow around images, and size your images manually on your home page. I'll show you how to set these options with Hotdog. Then explain them individually.

III

Spicing It Up!

Using Hotdog to Set Image Options

Earlier this chapter you saw how to use Hotdog to add a simple image to your HTML document. There is also a second Hotdog command that allows you to choose your advanced image placement characteristics from different menus.

To bring up the advanced image placing tools, choose **Insert**, **Image (Advanced)** from the Hotdog menu bar to bring up the image properties dialog box (see fig. 5.10).

Fig. 5.10

I can add my image and set all the options in one step with this dialog box.

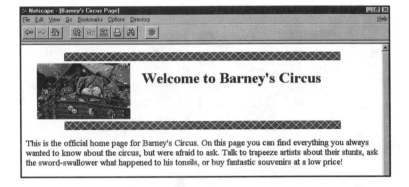

Here's a quick run-down of the different boxes available to you from this screen (see table 5.2). Read the following sections to understand these options thoroughly and see examples on using them.

Table 5.2   Available Boxes on the Hotdog Screen

Option	Action
IMAGE FILE	Same as before, the file name and path to your image.
Low-Resolution Image File	Lets you choose an image that is less detailed to appear first before your regular image is displayed. Rarely used unless you have gigantic images in your home page.
Alternate Description	The text that appears in the ALT keyword.
Width Height Horizontal Distance from Text	How wide your image is (WIDTH keyword). Your picture's height (HEIGHT keyword). Setting that lets you separate your text and images by a certain space (set in pixels).
Vertical Distance from Text	Same as above, only controls the vertical distance.

Option	Action
Border Width	Lets you create a black border around your image. Useful in framing your images.
Alignment	Allows you to choose values allowed with the ALIGN keyword.

Choose your settings and **click** on the **OK** button. Hotdog will add the HTML tag and all your settings for you.

Note

Hotdog is only useful for setting your image options when you first add the image to your home page. To make changes after that, you've got to manually edit your HTML. The following sections explain the required HTML to set each option.

Providing Alternative Text

Some browsers don't support both GIF and JPEG, while others don't support any images at all. Although Netscape supports both of these popular image types, you can tell it not to load any images when browsing WWW pages so you don't have to spend lots of time downloading them.

Tip

To tell Netscape not to automatically load images for every Web page it visits, choose Options, Auto Load Images from the menu bar. Choose it again to toggle image loading back on.

To accommodate these situations, it is a common courtesy to always provide alternative text descriptions to the images you include on your home page. Alternative text is part of the <IMG> tag. You add the **ALT=** keyword to your tag and type text inside the quotation marks. If I add alternative text to my TIGERS.GIF example used above, my new tag looks like this:

```
<IMG SRC=TIGERS.GIF ALT=Barneys Tigers>
```

If I turn off image loading in Netscape, or view the page with a browser that doesn't recognize GIF files, people will see Barney's Tigers where the image should appear. Figure 5.11 shows how alternative text appears on WWW pages.

III

Spicing It Up!

Fig. 5.11
Heres how images
are displayed
when Netscape
users choose not
to load them.

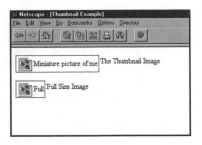

Tip

You can add alternative text with the insert image dialog box. Type in alternative text below your image's file name.

Aligning Your Image

When you place images on your home page, you have several different options for how they align themselves on the screen with respect to text on your page. Netscape recognizes the ALIGN keyword as part of the <IMG> tag.

With ALIGN, you have control over where the image is placed on screen and how text appears around it. You have eight different ALIGN options, as listed in table 5.3:

Table 5.3   Image Alignment Table

Option	Action
LEFT	Lines the image up on the left hand side of the page with multiple lines of text wrap around the side of the image on the right.
RIGHT	Just like LEFT, except the image appears on the right hand side of the page.
TOP	Aligns the image to the tallest item on the line.
TEXTTOP	Aligns the image to the tallest text item on the line (usually appears the exact same as TOP).
MIDDLE	Aligns the bottom of your line of text with the middle of the image.
ABSMIDDLE	Aligns the middle of your line of text with the middle of the image (very similar to MIDDLE, but used for small images).
BOTTOM	Aligns the bottom of your line of text to the bottom of the image.
BASELINE	Identical to BOTTOM.

Since they're very similar to the other keywords, I wouldn't bother using TEXTTOP, ABSMIDDLE, and BASELINE in your home page; they'll just confuse you in the long run.

Caution

Only Netscape recognizes the LEFT, RIGHT, TEXTTOP, ABSMIDDLE, and BASELINE keywords in the <IMG> tag. Other browsers do recognize the TOP, MIDDLE, and BOTTOM keywords though. If you use the Netscape alignment keywords, remember that your page will format differently in other browsers.

To set your image's alignment to be LEFT, add ALIGN=LEFT to your <IMG> tag. Now, your tiger image tag looks like this:

    <IMG SRC=TIGERS.GIF ALT=Barneys Tigers ALIGN=LEFT>

Now my text appears to the right of the tiger image as in figure 5.12.

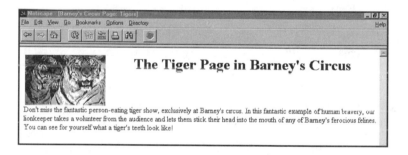

Fig. 5.12
Using the ALIGN tag lets you control where your image is placed.

Note

When using the LEFT and RIGHT keywords, you might want to also add the Netscape enhanced <BR> tag to your HTML document. You can add <BR CLEAR=LEFT> and <BR CLEAR=RIGHT> to make sure that text appearing after the image appears below the image instead of next to it. Since I only wanted the headline (The Tiger Page in Barneys Circus) to appear next to the text, I had to use the <BR CLEAR=LEFT> tag.

Sizing Your Image

Besides aligning your image, you can also manually control the height and width images appear on your page. Normally, Netscape displays the image in its regular size, but with the HEIGHT and WIDTH keywords you can shrink or enlarge an image's appearance without altering the actual image.

III

Spicing It Up!

Defining the image's height and width speeds up page browsing because Netscape can save a place for the image on your screen while loading the rest of your home page's text. You must define the HEIGHT and WIDTH of how the image should appear in pixels, thus limiting the size of the picture on-screen.

Note

A pixel (picture element) is a unit of measurement that's used to calculate monitor resolution. To get an idea of how large a pixel is, consider that a standard VGA screen is 640 (Width) by 480 (Height) pixels. Super VGA is 800 by 600 pixels. Thus an image that is of 320x240 pixels in dimension would take up approximately half a VGA screen.

Add the HEIGHT and WIDTH keywords to your <IMG> tag the same way you add the alignment and alternative text keywords. Unfortunately, you've got to add these keywords to your home page manually, without Hotdog help. To add height and width keywords to my TIGERS.GIF picture, the HTML code would look like:

<IMG SRC=TIGERS.GIF ALT=Barneys Tigers ALIGN=LEFT WIDTH=175 HEIGHT=110>

The TIGERS.GIF is now set to appear at the pre-defined size of 175 pixels across your screen and 110 pixels tall.

Actually, setting the HEIGHT and WIDTH keywords is another useful way for controlling the appearance size of an image on your home page. You could add an image to your home page and use smaller HEIGHT and WIDTH dimensions to make it appear thumbnail size. Figure 5.13 shows how you can change the appearance of the same image into several different sizes.

Fig. 5.13
Each image is proportionally twice as large as the next.

Adding Icons to Your Home Page

Besides adding full color images and pictures to your home page, you can also place all sorts of icons in it as well. While icons technically fall under the term images (they're GIF and JPEG files as well), they are typically extremely small (2-6K) and are used for design, aesthetic, and navigational purposes on home pages.

Icons come in many shapes and sizes. Ranging from miniature construction icons to colorful lines and buttons, you'll see a wide variety of them on pages across the WWW. Oftentimes you won't even realize that you're looking at icons when you browse a home page because they're so well integrated in the design.

I've included a vast array of icons on the home page CD. I can practically guarantee that you'll find several icons that will look great on your home page. I'm going to take you on a brief tour of some of these icons and show you some uses for them on your home page.

Lines and Bars

In chapter 3 I explained how to use the <HR> tag to separate pieces of your Web page. It's also extremely popular to use simple graphics of lines and bars to replace the <HR> tag.

Line graphics exist in all shapes, colors, and designs, and are significantly different than using the <HR> tag. See figure 5.14 for an example of how I use the file REDBAR.GIF instead of the <HR> tag on the circus home page. You can find this graphic in the /GRAPHICS/ICONS/LINES sub-directory on the CD-ROM.

The page is more attractive, colorful, and fits better with the circus theme. Below is the HTML code added—actually, I've added the same HTML twice; that's how the same bar appears in two different spots.

```
<CENTER><IMG SRC="redbar.gif"></CENTER>
```

Bullets

Bullets are commonly used to replace the dots that appear when you add an unordered list to your home page. You'll find bullets of all sorts of colors and sizes in the /GRAPHICS/ICONS/BULLETS sub-directory on the CD-ROM.

III

Spicing It Up!

Fig. 5.14
Here's the circus home page with graphics and a line added.

Graphical line

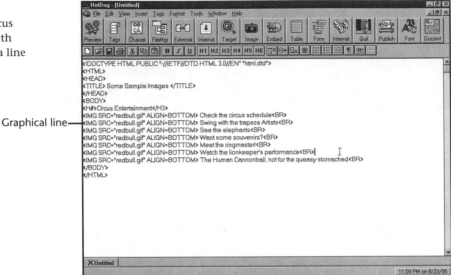

When I use bullets, I usually skip using an unordered list in my home page. Instead, I add each list item and then put the <BR> tag after it. The overall effect is a simulated list with neat icons serving as the bullets instead of the unordered list circles and squares.

Here's a sample of the HTML code I use to add graphical bullets to the circus home page.

> **Tip**
>
> Make sure you use the ALIGN keyword when placing bullets on your home page to ensure that your text lines up with the image correctly.

"New" Icons

Many sites also use icons to label new additions to their home page. This helps visitors quickly locate recent changes and information since their last visit. A whole stack of New icons can be found in the /GRAPHICS/ICONS/NEW sub-directory on the CD-ROM. See how the circus home page used the New icon (and bullets) in figure 5.15.

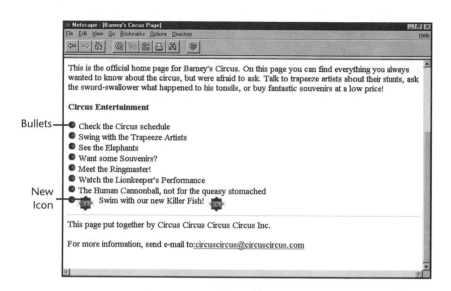

Fig. 5.15
Here's the spiffed up circus page, bullets and all.

Tip

Make sure you don't leave a new icon on your page for months and months. It's common practice to label a new item on your home page for the first month or so it's on there. After that, ditch the new icon for that item.

Construction Icons

Construction icons became popular awhile ago, when everybody's home page was new, and constantly being modified. These cute icons labeled the Web page as changing often, or not yet finished.

Nowadays, they're not quite as common, but you still see them on new pages regularly. You can dig through the icons in the /GRAPHICS/ICONS/CON-STRUCT sub-directory on the home page CD.

Navigation Icons

Navigation icons are probably the most useful icons to professional HTML developers, and least useful to people creating a basic home page. They come in handy when you have a large Web site with lots of pages linked together. Since your home page is likely to be simple, you may not find navigation icons to be very useful.

III

Spicing It Up!

These types of icons usually come in the form of arrows pointing one way or another. These arrows allow you to symbolize which way to go to bring up the next Web page. For example, if you were reading a book on the WWW, you'd probably see three icons on each page, a left arrow, right arrow, and a home icon. The left arrow would bring you to the preceding page, the right arrow brings up the next page, while the home icon would take you to the very beginning of the book. This saves you the trouble of picking your way through the back and forward buttons on the Netscape toolbar.

Navigation icons are really only useful if you are trying to tie together multiple pages at a site. See chapter 8, "Advanced and Cool Ways to Customize Your Home Page," for more ideas on using navigation icons on your pages. Check out the /GRAPHICS/ICONS/NAVIGATE sub-directory on the home page CD for lots of unique navigational icons.

Give Your Home Page Some Background

One of the neatest features of Netscape's extensions to HTML is the ability to control what the background of your document looks like. Instead of creating pages that only have the standard gray color behind text, you can change the background to any color you wish. If you still aren't happy with the plain color, Netscape also lets you place images behind your text to add a lot of color, texture, and fun to your home page.

Adding Background Colors

A long time ago, people weren't too choosy with the kind of car they drove. Everyone drove a Ford Model T, which only came in black. That car suited several generations of people until it dawned on buyers that cars can come in any color and shape they imagined. Nowadays when you're driving down the road, you can see cars ranging from neon purple to iguana green—variety enough for everyone's taste.

Colorizing home pages evolved in the same fashion. Originally, all home pages had a white or gray background because that's how viewers like Mosaic and Netscape displayed them. After awhile, people started becoming bored with the status quo, and Netscape created the BGCOLOR keyword to change the background color of any home page on the WWW. With the BGCOLOR tag, you literally have 16,777,216 background colors to choose from. That's all the colors of the rainbow, and then some.

The BGCOLOR keyword is added to the standard HTML <BODY> tag that surrounds most of your home page text. You add BGCOLOR=#rrggbb, where rrggbb is an alpha-numeric combination of mixing shades of red, green, and blue (like mixing paint to find that perfect color).

> **Tip**
>
> For a fantastic list of many useful background colors, stop by **http://www.infi.net/wwwimages/colorindex.html** and see over 100 choice red, blue, and green combinations.

Using Background Images

Besides standard colors, you can also add customized background images to your home page. These patterned graphics can give a cool effect to your home page when used properly. Background patterns consist of itsy-bitsy GIF images that are tiled next to each other so they cover your entire background (it's like wallpapering your Netscape background with a colorful GIF). Your text and images are placed on top of the background image.

Background patterns are added in the same way you change the background color, only they use the BACKGROUND keyword. Simply add BACKGROUND=YOUR.GIF to your <BODY> tag, and Netscape will load your image automatically. You'll find hundreds of sample background images on the home page CD. Here's how I used the background BD.JPG in the circus page (see fig. 5.16):

```
<BODY BACKGROUND= BD.JPG >
```

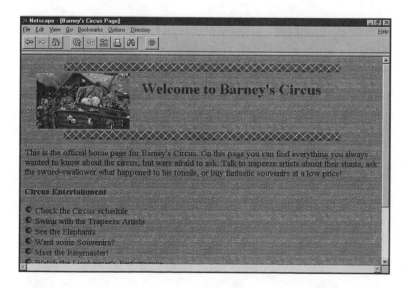

Fig. 5.16
Background patterns add a lot of texture to home pages.

III

Spicing It Up!

Background Problems

Before you go hog wild with using background colors and patterns, it's important to keep some issues in mind.

Many careless uses of colors and patterns end up with the original page becoming absolutely unreadable. Some Web creators choose a dark color, or a really busy background pattern, and it is virtually impossible to read text on those types of pages. As a good general rule of thumb, use only light colors, and calm, easy-to-read backgrounds for your home page. And above all, make sure you check out each page and make sure they are readable.

> **Note**
>
> You can also change the color that text appears on your home page. This flexibility allows you to use an extremely dark background, and very light text. Changing text color works the same way as changing the background color, only it uses the TEXT keyword. Add TEXT=#rrggbb to your <BODY> tag and pick any text color you want.

Second, adding background images to a home page can considerably increase the amount of time it takes for visitors to read your page. All the background images on the home page CD are reasonable to use size-wise. If you use other background patterns, or make your own, make sure you limit them to a maximum of 10K.

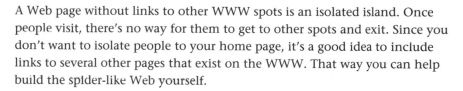

Chapter 6

Linking Web Pages Together

A Web page without links to other WWW spots is an isolated island. Once people visit, there's no way for them to get to other spots and exit. Since you don't want to isolate people to your home page, it's a good idea to include links to several other pages that exist on the WWW. That way you can help build the spider-like Web yourself.

In the last chapter, you learned how to combine graphical images with your home page. Now that you're familiar with using images, icons, and background graphics on your Web page, it's time to take the next step and learn to link different pages on the WWW together.

Linking Web pages together is the most basic feature of the WWW. Any document can contain a link to another WWW document with a special HTML tag. This chapter is all about using these hypertext link tags to connect Web pages to one another. You'll learn the proper way to link your home page to other HTML documents anywhere on the Internet.

Specifically, in this chapter you learn how to:

- Understand and dissect an HTML link
- Link your home page to another WWW page
- Make your images serve as links
- Organize and keep track of your links
- Avoid common linking pitfalls

Understanding Hypertext Links

As a Web surfer, you've probably already experienced hypertext links on the Web pages you've seen. While scanning through a page, you notice some text appears in blue, and is underlined. Text displayed like this is labeled hot because clicking on it links you automatically to another Web page.

Every URL requires three parts, a protocol, Internet site, and file and path name. In this chapter, I talk about http, the default WWW protocol (a protocol is the way two computers speak to each other). You must supply the Internet site and file and path name.

For example, my home page URL is:

http://www.cis.ohio_state.edu//shafran

Translated into English, this means use the special WWW communication method (http) to connect to the Internet through computers at Ohio State. Then find Andy's home page in his own directory (~shafran).

Hypertext links are often used because they can transparently join two documents on opposite sides of the world. Documents and files on the Internet are referred to by their own unique address, called URL (Uniform Resource Locator). To link two documents to each other, home page designers insert a URL into their Web pages. Using a URL is like addressing e-mail. The Internet computers understand how to translate the URL and find the exact spot to connect to.

If the home page is in New York, it doesn't matter if the linked document is in the Bronx, or New Zealand, the WWW treats it the same way. Netscape uses each URL to find documents on the Internet and bring them up automatically for you. As a Web surfer, you don't have to worry about using URLs, connecting to Internet sites around the world, or locating the correct document, Netscape takes care of all that hassle for you.

With the WWW, you can link to HTML documents (your home page), files (via FTP), Internet Newsgroups (like UseNet), and even popular information sources such as Gopher and the Wide Area Information Server directly from your home page.

For more information on these Internet features and how to use them on your home page, see "Linking to Other Internet Resources" in chapter 8.

> **Note**
>
> This chapter teaches you how to link HTML documents to each other. See "Linking to Other Internet Information" in chapter 8 for instructions on using the other popular Internet protocols in your home page.

On your home page, every link must be created one at a time. You get to decide what text to make hot, and more importantly, where you want to link the hot text to. You can add as many (or few) links to your home page as you like and organize them in any fashion.

Anatomy of a Link

Linking Web pages to each other isn't very difficult, but you've got to understand the HTML syntax and how to add links to your home page.

Just like every other HTML element, links have their own HTML tag. This tag (called the anchor tag—<A>) lets you specify which file you are linking to, what text should be hot or underlined when viewing your home page through Netscape, and then concluded with the closing tag (</A>).

Here's an example of what a link on my home page looks like in HTML:

```
                              ┌ URL
Anchor tag—<A HREF=http://www.mcp.com/que/>Que Publishing</A>————Closing anchor tag
            │                                    │
  Hypertext reference keyword              Text highlighted
```

Figure 6.1 shows how the same link appears in my home page

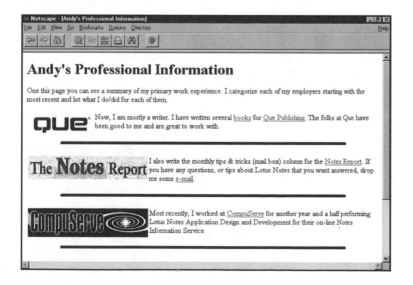

Fig. 6.1
Since *Que Publishing* is hot text, it appears underlined.

III

Spicing It Up!

Creating a Link

Now that you've read about using links and have seen them in action, let's add one to your home page. We will add two different (but similar) kinds of links to your home page.

First, I am going to show you how to link local documents to your home page. A local document is one which is at the same Internet location as your home page. Local documents are easier to link to because you don't have to know the complete URL, only its file name and path relative from your home page.

Using almost the identical process, you'll also learn to link documents together when they are located at different spots on the WWW. For this type of link you need to add the entire URL to your home page.

Linking to Local Web Pages

Oftentimes you will have multiple HTML documents in one spot. There may be too much information to put in one document, so you split it up into several different HTML files. In your main Web page, you want to link to each of those separate documents easily and quickly. Maybe your home page is set up like a table of contents, linking to several different pages.

Only the text `Tiger Exhibit` appears on my circus home page. I'll add another example link for the elephant exhibit as well. We will add a link to the tiger exhibit using Hotdog. The first step is typing the text you want highlighted as a link to your page. I'll type **Tiger Exhibit** on my circus page. Then select and highlight that text with your mouse and click on the **file manger icon** to bring up the Hotdog file manager dialog box (see fig. 6.2).

Fig. 6.2
The built-in file manager lets you link your home page to any document you select.

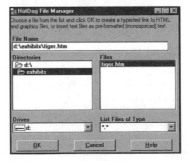

Using the mouse, I'll select the file I want to link to. I'm going to select **TIGERS.HTM** from the EXHIBITS sub-directory. Then click **OK** to add the link. Hotdog creates the HTML link automatically:

<A HREF="exhibits\tiger.htm">Tiger Exhibit</A>

See figure 6.3 for how the new circus home page looks once I've added the two animal links.

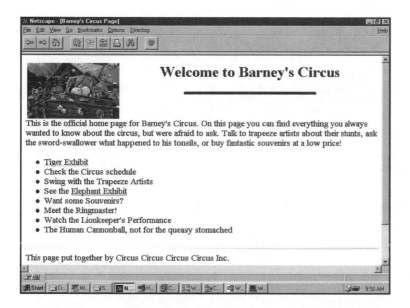

Fig. 6.3
Here's the circus home page with the new links added.

> **Caution**
>
> When you set up local file links while creating your home page on your PC, remember to keep the same file name and path structure when you upload your files to your WWW site. If I forget to create an Exhibits sub-directory on my Internet site, Netscape won't be able to properly find the linked file.

Linking Elsewhere on the WWW

You'll also want to learn how to link your home page to other HTML documents that reside on other WWW sites besides your own. Linking to these sites requires you to know the full URL to the document, not just the file name and path as in the above example.

III

Spicing It Up!

The link, however, looks the same. You still use the <A HREF=> and </A> tags to surround hot text. When you are linking to other HTML documents on the Web, your URL will always start with

HTTP://

That's so Netscape knows how to display the Hypertext document properly. The rest of the URL consists of the Internet path of the site, and then the full name of the document you are linking to.

> ### Tip
>
> By default, if you don't specify a file name, Netscape automatically loads the file INDEX.HTML when you link to a site. Since it is a WWW standard, nearly every site has an INDEX.HTML file. At my site, my home page is named index.html.

As an example, I'm going to add a link to the Yahoo list of WWW circuses (there's not many) to Barney's Circus Page.

Choose **Insert**, **Simple URL** from the Hotdog menu bar to bring up the insert URL dialog box shown in figure 6.4.

Fig. 6.4
Hotdog lets you insert a URL in the same fashion as you added a graphic in the last chapter.

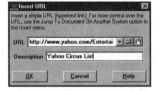

Type in the full URL of the HTML document you are linking to in the URL box. The URL of the Yahoo Circus List is:

http://www.yahoo.com/Entertainment/Miscellaneous/Circus/

Then type in the text that will appear hot in Netscape in the description box:

Yahoo Circus List

When you are finished, click **OK** to add the link to your document. The following line of HTML was added to the circus home page:

<A HREF="http://www.yahoo.com/Entertainment/Miscellaneous/Circus/">Yahoo Circus List</A>

With the link added, you can easily jump from one page to another as shown in figures 6.5 and 6.6.

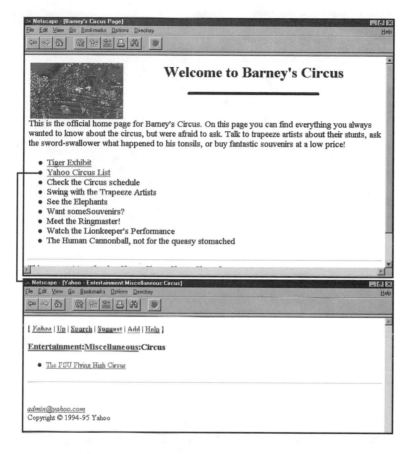

Fig. 6.5
Clicking on the link in the circus home page brings up the linked document.

Fig. 6.6
The linked document.

Using Images as Links

Not only can you use text to link to other WWW pages, but you can use images as well. In the last chapter, I explained how to add images to your home page. Now you'll learn how to make them "clickable." That's when you click your mouse on an image and a separate WWW document is linked to and appears.

You can link an image on your home page to another HTML document in the exact same fashion as you linked text. The only difference is that instead of designating text to be hot, you are assigning an image instead. In Netscape, a blue box appears around the image and links visitors to a different page when they click their mouse anywhere on the picture. You can use any kind of image, picture, or icon except for background images to link WWW documents together.

Tip

Using images to link pages together is very common. But make sure you use recognizable images so that visitors know where they will link to. For example, if you are going to link your home page to a list of your favorite songs, use an icon that is music related. It's also extremely important to use the ALT keyword when linking images. This ensures that visitors that can't see images will be able to use your links from page to page.

I link several graphics in my home page to different Web sites. For example, I have the *Que* logo displayed prominently in the list of my past and present employers. I'd like to have the logo linked to the publisher's home page so that if you click on it, you'll immediately be brought to the *Que* site on the WWW.

This link is the exact same as the one I used at the very beginning of the chapter with one change. Instead of typing *Que Publishing* between the link tags, the HTML code for displaying an image is there instead. Below is the HTML code and figure 6.7 shows how the newly linked image appears.

<A HREF="http://www.mcp.com/que/">

<IMG SRC="gifs/quelogo.gif"ALIGN=LEFT>

</A>

Fig. 6.7
Now the *Que* logo is wired from my home page.

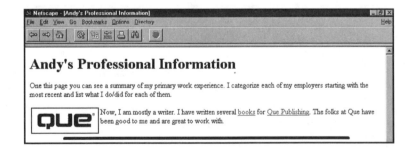

> **Note**
>
> With some more advanced HTML programming, you can also create clickable imagemaps that take you to different pages depending on where in the image you selected. These types of graphics are called imagemaps and are significantly more complicated to create and maintain. For more information about using imagemaps, see "Explaining Image Maps" in chapter 9.

Using Anchors on Your Home Page

Now that you're an accomplished HTML linker, you can connect your home page to any other file on the Internet. However, there are a few other uses for the <A> and </A> anchor tags, notably using them as internal document references and pointers.

Here's what I mean. Let's say you picked up a large book because you wanted to read the contents of chapter 26. You don't want to have to flip through and scan the first 25 chapters just to locate chapter 26 in your book. Instead, you'd go to the table of contents, find out what page chapter 26 begins on, and go straight there.

Anchor tags work in a similar way. When you have a large HTML document, you can add anchors to various points in the document. In this example, if the large book was one *really* big HTML file, you'd probably have an anchor at the beginning of each chapter. At the very beginning of the HTML file, you'd have a table of contents that would link to each separate anchor in your file (one for each chapter). By clicking on the one labeled chapter 26, Netscape would take you automatically to where the chapter 26 anchor is in the same file. You wouldn't have to scroll through countless pages of information.

Pretty nifty, huh? Anchors work the same way as linking to other documents on the WWW, except that you are linking to internal spots of a single document instead. Just like regular links, you can have as many anchors and tags as you wish, but don't go overboard.

These anchor tags are called targets by Hotdog when used as references like this. I use anchor tags on my home page. At the top of the page, there are several different areas in which I have organized my interests. Clicking on any of those pieces of hot text takes you to a different part of my home page. Of course you could also get there by simply scrolling down the page, but by having a table of contents at the top, you can instantly go to the area of my home page you were looking for.

My tags are labeled to break my page into four different parts: Personal Information, Professional Information, Academic Information, and Publications. Let me show you how I added my anchor tags, and how Hotdog helps me manage and link to them.

Note

Instead of using the name anchors, many people also split their home page into many separate pages. See "Making Your Home Page a Home Site" in chapter 8 for more information on how to do that.

Originally, I used anchors in my home page (and through this example), but eventually I split my home page up. When you visit, you won't see any anchors there now.

Creating and Naming an Anchor

On your home page, you can add named anchor tags wherever you like. Each tag you add will allow you to jump directly to that spot with a link. For this example, I have four different anchor tags and links in my home page.

In HTML, anchors use the following format:

<A NAME="Named Anchor"> Anchor text displayed </Λ>

To dissect the above line, I am adding an anchor tag around **Anchor text displayed**. To jump to this tag, I must link to the target labeled **Named Anchor.**

Hotdog lets you add anchors to your page easily. Highlight the text you want to mark as an anchor, and click on the **Target** icon to bring up the Enter Target ID dialog box shown in figure 6.8. I'm going to highlight one of my main four headings talking about my professional information:

<H1>Andy's Professional Information</H1>

Tip

You don't have to place your target around text if you don't wish to. In that case, don't highlight any text, just move your cursor to the spot you'd like the target to be added, then click on the Target icon.

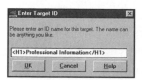

Fig. 6.8
Place your target/
anchor label here.

Type the name of your anchor and click **OK**. I'll type **Professional Information** for my home page. The following lines of HTML appear:

    <A NAME="Professional Information">

    <H1>Andy's Professional Information</H1>

    </A>

There's now an anchor on my home page at the beginning of the section that lists my professional information.

> **Tip**
>
> Make sure that you put the anchor tag at the very top of where you want to jump, because Netscape places the line with the anchor at the very top of its screen. If your anchor is below your headline, you wouldn't see it when you jumped to that spot (you could scroll up and see it though).

Linking to an Anchor

Once you have created all of the anchors on your home page, it's time to create your own Table of Contents, or links to each specific target.

Go to the top of your home page in Hotdog and click on the **Internal icon** at the top of the screen to bring up the select hypertext target dialog box shown in figure 6.9.

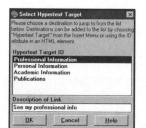

Fig. 6.9
All of the targets
in this HTML
document are
listed here.

Choose the target you want to link to in the **Hypertext Target ID** box and type the text that will link you to that target in the **Description of Link** box. When you are finished, click **OK** and Hotdog will add your HTML link for you:

<A HREF="#Professional Information">

See my professional info

</A>

Notice the # in the HREF keyword? That symbol tells Netscape to look for a target instead of a separate HTML document. Netscape displays the hot text just like any other link (see fig. 6.10). But instead of looking for a different file, or going to a separate WWW site, Netscape looks only in the HTML file it is displaying for the named anchor.

Fig. 6.10
My home page now has anchors and links added to it.

Note

You can link directly to anchors in any HTML document on the WWW. So if you wanted to create a link on your home page to the Professional Information anchor on my home page, you'd add the following piece of HTML to your home page:

<A HREF="http://www.cis.ohio-state.edu/~shafran#Professional Information">

Link to Andy's info

</A>

To link to a specific target on another page, view the HTML source code of that document (in Netscape, choose **View**, **Source** from the menu bar) and find the target you want to link into.

Caution

Linking to anchors is often not a good idea. They tend to change often. Remember, I removed all the anchors on my page already.

Organize Your Links with Lists

Now that you've started using links in your home page, it's important to keep them organized so that they're understandable and easy to use. It's easy to let your links get unorganized and fall into disarray. Every time you add new HTML to your home page, you need to make sure that the page is easy to read and organized.

One popular method for keeping your links organized is using a list. As you learned previously in chapter 4, lists help present many different pieces of information in a crisp, bulleted format. Lists work perfectly when you want to include a bunch of links on your home page. For example, almost everyone has their own personal compilation of neat WWW pages (I have one). On my list, there are many of the popular places that I like to visit when I am browsing the Web. If they weren't in list format, my links would be a jumbled mess and unusable.

To create an unordered list of links, all you have to do is use the standard <UL>, <LI>, and </UL> tags. Let each link use a separate <LI> tag so that you have only one link per line. I guarantee that a simple list will do more for organizing a bunch of links than practically any other way you could organize your page. See figure 6.11 for how I use a list to organize my hotlinks:

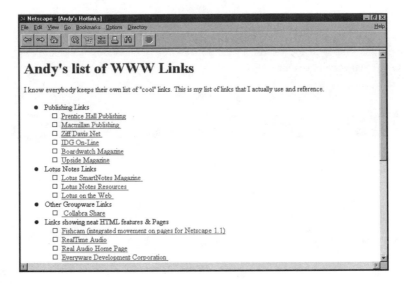

Useful Linking Tips

Knowing how to add WWW links on your home page adds a powerful dimension to your HTML authoring repertoire. Along with this increased power and flexibility comes the opportunity to make your home page much more confusing and difficult to use for people who stop by for a visit.

Here's a list of some of important issues to remember when adding links to your home page. Some of them seem like common sense, others might be more obscure. Just by following this short set of tips, you won't have to worry about making your page more confusing when you start adding links to your home page.

Don't Over Link

Nothing is more confusing than stopping by a Web page with 200 words of text and 180 of them are linked to different spots on the WWW (like in figure 6.12). Since linked text appears underlined and in blue, having too many links in a paragraph (or page) makes it completely unreadable. No one will want to stop by.

Visiting various Web pages is a lot like window shopping. If you see a store that has an absolutely hideous and cluttered front window, you're probably less inclined to stop by and shop. Keep this in mind when adding links to your home page. If you have so many different links you want to include, consider adding a simple (but organized) list to the bottom of your page.

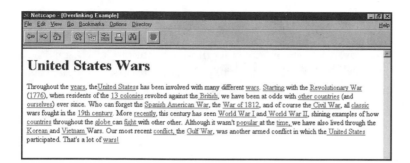

Fig. 6.12
I get a headache just looking at this page

Link Specific/Descriptive Words

Although the WWW relies on links that connect pieces of information with each other, try to make your links transparent. Here's an example of what I mean. The following paragraph does NOT have a transparent link (I marked the links in **bold**):

> Barney's Circus is a barrel full of fun. Individuals and families of all ages and backgrounds can come to the circus and enjoy themselves. Click on **Barney's Circus** to see a picture of what the big top tent looks like. The tent is world famous as the tallest tent being used today.

Try this text instead:

> Barney's Circus is a barrel full of fun. Individuals and families of all ages and backgrounds can come to the circus and enjoy themselves. You won't want to miss the **big top tent** to see the world's tallest tent still in use today.

Your links shouldn't interrupt the flow of text as they did in the first example. You can assume that readers implicitly know that underlined text will bring them to a related area.

Caution

One of my largest criticisms of Web page creators is that they often highlight useless pieces of text as the link to another Web site. Of course the most notorious culprit is the word **here**. You should NEVER, EVER have the word **here** highlighted as the text that links your visitors to another page.

Even if you don't use **here** as hot text on your page, you still need to be careful when choosing text to link to other pages. One common way that I use to decide if I have accurately labeled my link is imagining that my home page is only displayed as linked text. Then I decide if I understand what information will appear if I click on a link by its name alone, without the context of the rest of the sentence.

III

Spicing It Up!

Describe Large Links

Whenever you link your home page to larger graphics, files, audio bites, or video clips (even extremely large text files), you should let visitors know about the potential file size *before* they click on the link. Large files take a while to download. I'll talk more about this in the next chapter.

Keep Your Links Current

As you get more experienced and continue to build your home page, you're likely to compile an entire collection of links to various parts of the Web. Occasionally, these links become obsolete. The Web page may be deleted or move to another site. Whatever the reason, you've got a decent chance that some of your links will become obsolete every few months.

Visitors who stop by and see a neat link will be using the link provided in your home page, only to find that the Web page you've linked to no longer exists. If you are going to have links on your home page, you should periodically check them all to make sure they are pointing to current documents. Otherwise, you shouldn't have them on your home page.

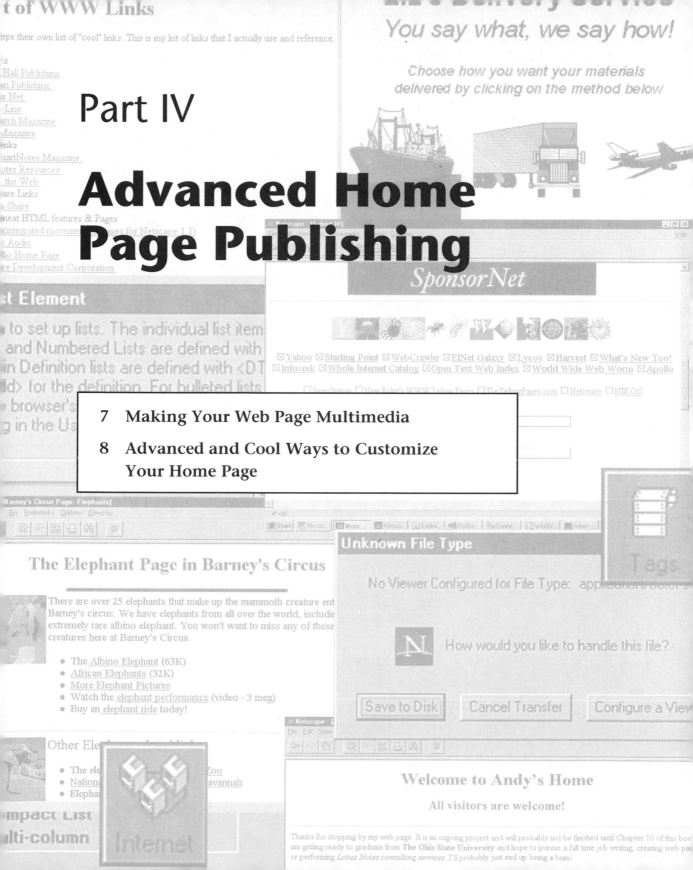

Part IV

Advanced Home Page Publishing

st of WWW Links

...eeps their own list of "cool" links. This is my list of links that I actually use and reference.

...nks
...e Hall Publishing
...llan Publishing
...vis Net
...On-Line
...watch Magazine
...e Magazine
... Links
...SmartNotes Magazine
...Notes Resources
...on the Web
...ware Links
...ora Share
...ng neat HTML features & Pages
...m (integrated movement on pages for Netscape 1.1)
...me Audio
...udio Home Page
...ware Development Corporation

ist Element

...en to set up lists. The individual list item...
..., and Numbered Lists are defined with...
...s in Definition lists are defined with <DT...
...<dd> for the definition. For bulleted lists,...
...he browser's default bullets with your ov...
...ng in the Use Image field.

You say what, we say how!

Choose how you want your materials
delivered by clicking on the method below

SponsorNet

⊠Yahoo ⊠Starting Point ⊠WebCrawler ⊠EINet Galaxy ⊠Lycos ⊠Harvest ⊠What's New Too!
⊠Infoseek ⊠Whole Internet Catalog ⊠Open Text Web Index ⊠World Wide Web Worm ⊠Apollo

☐JumpStation ☐New Rider's WWW Yellow Pages ☐TheYellowPages.com ☐Netcenter ☐NIKOS

Title:

URL:
http://

Category:
Health & Fitness   If Other, please Specify

Netscape - [Submit It!]
File Edit View Go Bookmarks Options Directory

Start ... Nets... ...

The Elephant Page in Barney's Circus

There are over 25 elephants that make up the mammoth creature ent...
Barney's circus. We have elephants from all over the world, includir...
extremely rare albino elephant. You won't want to miss any of these...
creatures here at Barney's Circus.

- The Albino Elephant (63K)
- African Elephants (32K)
- More Elephant Pictures
- Watch the elephant performance (video - 3 meg)
- Buy an elephant ride today!

Other Ele...

- The ele...Zoo
- Nationa...avannah
- Elepha...

...ompact List
...ulti-column

Unknown File Type

No Viewer Configured for File Type: application/oct...

How would you like to handle this file?

Save to Disk   Cancel Transfer   Configure a V...

Tags

Internet

Netscape - [
File Edit View

Welcome to Andy's Home

All visitors are welcome!

Thanks for stopping by my web page. It is an ongoing project and will probably not be finished until Chapter 10 of thi...
am getting ready to graduate from **The Ohio State University** and hope to pursue a full time job writing, creating we...
or performing *Lotus Notes consulting services*. I'll probably just end up being a bum!

Chapter 7

Making Your Web Page Multimedia

Imagine making the movie Star Wars. All George Lucas started with was a plain old text manuscript (which you can download at **http://www.books.com**). That manuscript may have been thorough, but it wasn't nearly as much fun as the actual movie. You needed the great soundtrack and cool special effects to make the movie fun and enjoyable. Without them, Star Wars would have been just like any other movie about intergalactic war.

While we aren't going to create Star Wars, you'll learn how you can add all sorts of special effects to your home page. Adding audio bites and sound clips is within your reach, and they'll separate your page from all the other text/image only pages out there.

So far, this book has taught you how you can mark your own corner of the Internet quickly and easily with a simple Web page. Now it's time to go that extra step and make your home page truly spectacular.

In chapter 5, I showed you how to add all sorts of images to your home page. With images, your home page became a multimedia page, because you combined graphics and text on one page. However, by today's terms, multimedia means including cool audio and video clips as part of your home page.

In this chapter you'll learn how to integrate audio bites and video clips onto your Web page to create a truly multimedia effect. Specifically, you'll learn how to:

- Browse the WWW for how other sites use multimedia

- Recognize the different audio and video file types available for your home page

- Start making your own audio and video clips
- Find existing multimedia clips on the home page CD and the Internet
- Add audio and video clips to your home page

A Sampling of Multimedia Sites

Althoughtechnically, your home page is multimedia because you use text and images, you won't qualify for a gold star unless you add audio or video clips to it (or possibly both). Before I show you how to use these new multimedia formats on your home page, let's take a look at how some other multimedia Web pages are set up. Several places on the Web integrate text, images, audio, and video clips on the same page to achieve startlingly good effects—and then there are those pages that you don't want your home page to look like.

Using all of these different media types presents several technical and design challenges. All of the design issues that came up when adding images to pages are now back, in threefold. You've got to worry about making these new aspects easy to use and have them naturally appear in your home page, without adding too much clutter and making your page unreadable.

On the technical side, creating and adding audio and video clips is no walk in the park. You've got to worry about file size, multi-platform compatibility (will PC, Mac, and UNIX users all be able to use the clips?), and the quality of the clip.

I'll talk about these issues and show you how to correctly add audio and video clips to your home page in this chapter.

Politically Correct Bedtime Stories

One of my favorite pages on the entire WWW is the home page for the book *Politically Correct Bedtime Stories*, by James Finn Garner (**http://www.mcp.com/general/news6/polit.html**). This site offers a simple, easy-to-use conglomeration of text, useful links, and enjoyable audio clips (see fig. 7.1). I can't wait for them to add the video!

The Brang Page

This page is a classic example of a Web page gone wrong. There are no explanations of what you are looking at, and you see confusing images and links to audio clips that you have no desire to hear. About the only points the Web page author would earn is for displaying the file size of his sound files.

Fig. 7.1
Simple and easy to use, this site is a model for a basic multimedia home page.

Stop by the Brang home page (**http://www.inch.com/~mick/home/ brang.html**) for a taste of a unique page (see fig. 7.2).

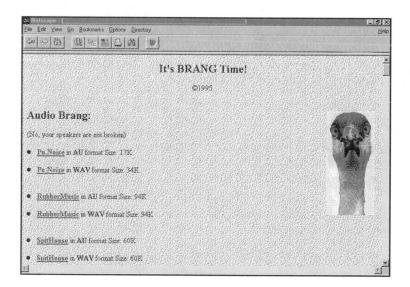

Fig. 7.2
This home page is difficult to read, use, and understand.

Great Multimedia Example—Star Trek Voyager

Another one of my favorite true multimedia sites is the Star Trek Voyager home page (**http://voyager.paramount.com/VoyagerActive.html**). This professionally designed page demonstrates what kind of Web page a lot of time and effort can create. I'm not really much of a trekkie, but there are so

Web Pages

many neat images, sounds, and video clips available on this site, its worth stopping by for a look (see fig. 7.3).

Fig. 7.3
Multimedia pages don't get much better than this. Crisp, clear instructions let you know exactly how to experience all the audio and video features.

Understanding and Using Audio Clips

Audio clips, sometimes referred to as sound bites, add another dimension to your home page. Not only can people see information you present, but they can hear it as well. Imagine watching Raiders of the Lost Ark without hearing the theme music, it just wouldn't be the same. Sound is a welcome addition to home pages because it makes them a lot more fun to explore.

Unlike adding images, when you put an audio clip on your home page, you are embedding an actual file that must be downloaded and played in separate steps. Images just appear alongside your text. Visitors who come to your home page choose which files to download and then play the audio clip on their computer subsequently.

> **Note**
>
> To hear audio clips on your computer, you need to have the correct hardware and software. If you are using a PC compatible machine, you must have a soundcard (preferably a SoundBlaster or compatible) and speakers hooked up. Most multimedia kits that come with CD-ROM drives include all the necessary hardware to hear sound clips. PC users also need audio software to actually hear their files being played. You can find a handful of audio players on the home page CD included with this book. Macintosh users on the other hand, have it even easier. Their multimedia capabilities are built in.

In this section I'll outline the different types of audio file formats and tell you where you can find your own audio clips to add to your home page.

Explain Audio File Types and Formats

Throughout the WWW, you'll see a wide variety of audio clip file types and formats. These formats represent the different methods used to electronically record the sounds into a computer. They all have their own advantages and common uses.

Choosing from the different file types is like picking the right kind of film for your camera. You can use 35mm, disc, 110, or even Polaroid's instant film. Each film type works differently in certain situations, but they all give you about the same results.

Primarily, there are three audio file formats to be familiar with (see table 7.1):

Table 7.1 Common Audio File Formats	
AU	Developed by Sun, this file format is called mu-law, and uses 8-bit sampling which makes the sounds crackle (like using a cordless phone), but offers reasonably acceptable quality. Recently, an 11 bit version of the AU audio format has started becoming more popular because it provides better quality. AU files tend to be small, compact, easy to download, and work on all types of computers. This file type is the 35mm film of the audio world. It's an international standard and works on just about every type of computer you can imagine.
.WAV	Microsoft Windows audio format. The .WAV extension is used for audio files created for use primarily under Microsoft Windows. While .WAV files tend to be of higher quality than the AU format (and also significantly larger file size), there can be some problems with listening to them on different types of computers.
AIFF	The Macintosh audio file format. Not very common on the Web, AIFF has the same limitations .WAV has for multi-computer compatibility.

The home page CD comes with programs that let you record and listen to any of these three file types, preparing you for virtually anything you'll find on the Web. See appendix C, "Home Page Final Checklist" for more information.

Web Pages

> **Tip**
>
> If you want to know more technical details about the audio file formats listed above (such as what 8 bit sampling really is), I would recommend reading the Audio File Format FAQ (Frequently Asked Questions) which can be found on the WWW at
> **http://www.cis.ohio-state.edu/hypertext/faq/usenet/audio-fmts/ top.html**

Where You Can Find Audio Clips

Now that you're familiar with the different types of audio clips, you'll probably want to add some to your home page. There are several different ways for you to obtain innovative and creative audio clips. Most people browse the WWW until they find audio clips that they like, others purchase the necessary equipment and digitize their own.

Included on the home page CD, you'll find several different sample audio files, in both AU and WAV formats. These audio files are meant to be a sampling of the kind you'll put in your home page.

> **Tip**
>
> Feel free to use the included AU and WAV audio clips in your home page however you like. You'll find a wide variety in the /AUDIO sub-directory on the CD-ROM.

Finding Audio Clips on the Internet

The Internet is a fantastic resource for music and audio clips of all sorts. You can download everything from Jim Carrey ("Allllrighty then") to Martin Luther King's "I Have a Dream" speech. Below, I've compiled a diverse list of popular WWW sites where you can find, download, and listen to audio clips. These are public archives that allow anyone to download their files:

- **http://sunsite.unc.edu/pub/multimedia/sun-sounds/movies/**
  This site has a fantastic set of movie sound clips from practically every movie you can remember. Some examples include snippets from: Bladerunner, Aliens, and the Raiders of the Lost Ark.

- **http://ai.eecs.umich.edu/people/kennyp/sounds.html**
  This is the most complete TV theme song site I have ever seen. If the show even had a pilot episode, you can find its theme song here. Stop by here to find everything from Mission Impossible to 60 Minutes.

- **http://Web.msu.edu/vincent/index.html**
  Famous people and speeches can be found here. I found Martin Luther King's "I Have a Dream" speech on this site.

- **http://www.acm.uiuc.edu/rml/**
  This is the most complete spot for digital audio and video clips that I could find. He includes links to hundreds of different multimedia sites around the web—a great place to explore!

Tip

When you click on audio files at these sites, Netscape automatically downloads them and plays them for you, without saving the file. Hold the **shift button** down when you click on **audio** (and video) **files** to save them permanently to your hard drive so you can listen to them and add them to your own home page.

Make Your Own Audio Clips

Finding neat audio clips on the WWW is fine for some people, but most of us want to have our own customized audio clips for our home page. Creating your own audio clips isn't too difficult or costly—it just requires a little bit of know-how.

Macintosh users have it easy. Nowadays, Macs come with multimedia capabilities and even their own microphones and software. You can speak directly to your Macintosh, have it record your speech, and put it on your home page within a few minutes. Make sure you save your audio file format in the AU file format (instead of Macs AIFF format)—AU is the most popular format on the WWW.

Don't fret if you are a PC owner though. Practically anyone who has a CD-ROM multimedia kit can create their own audio files nearly as easily. You can buy a cheap microphone (the Microsoft Sound System Kit comes with all the recording software and a microphone for under $50) to digitize your voice. For more advanced clips, you can connect your stereo directly into your sound card with a standard red/white cable.

Caution

Make sure you don't record sounds that you don't own. For example, you may really like the new U2 album, but digitizing it and making it available on your home page is illegal and could get you into hot water.

> **Note**
>
> I've just glossed over the process of recording your own audio clips here. Make sure you consult your system and multimedia manuals to learn how to digitize sounds properly on your specific computer. If you have trouble digitizing in AU format, the sound programs included on the home page CD will convert practically any sound format into the AU format.

Adding Audio Clips to Your Home Page

Actually, the hardest part to putting an audio clip on your home page is obtaining the right clip. Once you have an audio clip in hand, adding it to your home page is a breeze. You use the same HTML tags as you used to insert a link into your page, `<A HREF=>` and `</A>`.

On my home page, I wanted to add an audio welcome to visitors who stop by for the first time. After recording the greeting, I saved the file as **GREETING.AU**. To add it to my home page, I simply type the following lines of HTML:

<IMG SRC="images/sound.gif">

<A HREF="audio/GREETING.AU">Listen to my home page greeting (130K) </A>

The first line inserts a miniature *sound* icon which tells visitors that the link next to it is an audio file (see fig. 7.4). The second line is an actual HTML link to my sound file. Instead of displaying **GREETING.AU** in Netscape, a separate audio player will load and play the message when it is clicked upon.

Fig. 7.4
Now anyone can hear my voice!

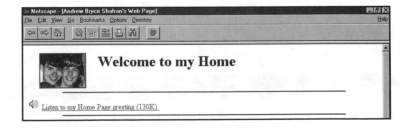

> **Note**
>
> Did you notice how I put the audio file size in parenthesis? That's so visitors to my Web page can estimate how long it will take to download the sound clip before they click on the link. As a common courtesy, you should list the file size of every audio and video file that you add to your home page.

Understanding and Using Video Clips

Adding audio clips to your home page is just the first step to making your home page a true multimedia experience. The next step is embedding video clips.

Video clips are combinations of movie pictures and sound bundled up together just like a movie. You can find video clips ranging from snippets of actual films to celebrity interviews. The range of video clips available is vast, though not nearly as large as the number of images and audio sounds available. Like adding audio clips to your home page, video clips are not played directly in Netscape. Home page visitors must download the clip and run a separate program to display the video clip on their computer.

Unfortunately, video clips have several drawbacks that can make them difficult to use. The main problem is file size. Video clips are gigantic, usually 1-2 megs in file size. That's because a video clip is a conglomeration of hundreds of images set to display one after another in rapid succession. Remember how I talked about image size in chapter 5? A one minute video clip can have as many as 1000 different image frames.

Downloading a 2 meg file, at the fastest speed your computer probably supports (28.8 baud) and in ideal conditions will still take 10-20 minutes. For the millions of WWW users using 14.4 or slower baud modems, the large file size often means that they won't spend the time downloading video clip.

> **Note**
>
> To view video clips on your computer, you must have the correct hardware and software. This includes enough RAM (8 megs minimum) on a Windows based computer to display the moving video images on-screen, and a video viewing program (several of which are included on the home page CD). Again, Macintosh readers are luckier, because they have these video capabilities built in.

Explaining Video File Types and Formats

There are several different types of video clips that you may run across when browsing on the Web. Currently, none of them reign supreme as the default video standard, so you have to decide which of the popular formats you want to use in your home page.

Primarily, there are three video file formats to be familiar with (see table 7.2):

Table 7.2 Common Video File Formats	
MPEG	One of the oldest video formats around, MPEG is similar to the JPEG image file format, only optimized for videos. The MPEG format is popular because video clips in this format tend to be of decent quality. Unfortunately, the MPEG format is hardware intensive and needs a lot of RAM and special hardware to create. Youll have to buy a special piece of equipment used to encode videos, and make sure youve got at least 16 megs of RAM.
AVI	Similar to the .WAV audio style, this is Microsoft's Video for Windows file format. Windows users can use AVI video files easily because they are optimized to be seen on a Windows computer. This video format is less popular than the other two, but still commonly used.
QT	QT, or Quicktime, is the video format developed and licensed by Apple Computer. Taking the WWW by storm, most new video clips are released in Quicktime format because it is multi-platform, compact file size, and easier to record with. My recommendation is to stick with the Quicktime format.

The home page CD comes with programs that let you watch virtually any type of video or animation clip that youll find on the Web. See appendix C, "Home Page Final Checklist" for more information.

Tip

If you want to know more technical details about the video formats listed above, try the following links:

MPEG—http://www.cis.ohio-state.edu/hypertext/faq/usenet/mpeg-faq/top.html

QT—http ://www.cast.uni-linz.ac.at/st/staff/rm/QTquickcam/

AVI—http://www.microsoft.com

Where You Can Find Video Clips

The same obstacle that presented itself with adding audio to your home page comes back two-fold for video clips. Finding high-quality and useful video clips that you want to add to your home page can be an extremely difficult task.

Included on the home page CD, youll find several different sample video clips in QT format. Take a look at how they work to get an idea of what kind of video clips you can use in your home page. The video clips are in the /VIDEO/ sub-directory on the CD-ROM.

Finding Video Clips on the Internet

There are several different WWW sites that have large collections of MPEG and QT movies. Downloading them all could take several weeks, but it's not a bad idea to stop by and pick up a few neat movie clips.

Heres a partial list of some hot spots to find good MPEG and QT files on the Web.

- **http://w3.eeb.ele.tue.nl/mpeg/index.html**
  A fantastic collection of movies in several different categories can be found here. Their video clips range from repairing the Hubble telescope to episodes of The Simpsons (quite a variety).

- **http://www.acm.uiuc.edu/rml/**
  This is the most complete spot for digital audio and video clips that I could find. As I mentioned above (in the audio clip section), this page has links to popular multimedia sites all over the WWW.

- **http://deathstar.rutgers.edu/people/bochkay/movies.html**
  An ever growing variety of Quicktime movies. Youll find different video clips that contain Kathy Ireland, Barney the Dinosaur, and Star Trek here.

Make Your Own Video Clips from Scratch

Just a year or two ago, if you had wanted to make your own video clips and put them on your home page, I would have strongly advised against it. At that point, the equipment required to digitize video and store it in electronic format was way too expensive and difficult to use.

Nowadays it's a different story. You have several affordable low cost alternatives to creating your own video clips. Basic video cameras that connect directly to your computer come with hardware and software for under $200.

You can also make video clips from VCR tapes that you already have. For about the same price range, you can purchase a digital converter which lets your VCR and computer talk to each other.

Stop by your local computer store to learn more about your digitizing options. By the way, most of the affordable software digitizes video into Quicktime format.

Adding Video Clips to Your Home Page

Video clips are just as easy to add to your home page as an audio clip was. You use the exact same tag, only you specify the video's file name instead.

In addition to my audio greeting, I have also digitized a video of myself welcoming visitors to my home page. After several takes on practicing to be Steven Spielberg, I finally created a decent video clip and named the file **WELCOME.QT**. Then I added a link to it in my home page with the following HTML:

> <IMG SRC="images/video.gif">

> <A HREF="video/WELCOME.QT">A video welcome to my home page (1.3 Meg) </A>

The first line inserts a miniature video icon which tells visitors that the link next to it is a video clip. The second line is an actual HTML link to my video clip. When clicked upon, visitors will download the Quicktime video clip, load a video player for their computer and watch the clip automatically (see fig. 7.5).

Fig. 7.5
With a little more practice, I can go to Hollywood.

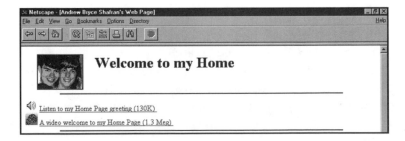

Chapter 8

Advanced and Cool Ways to Customize Your Home Page

Remember when you bought your last car? You went to the dealer's lot, haggled over a few bucks and drove off the lot. You had a nice car, but I'm sure you wanted to add a few personal (and cool) customizations to it. Some people add CD players or alarms, others add a sunroof or neon lights to their car—and you don't want to forget about the fuzzy dice! These personalized customizations are why every car is different and unique.

Right now, you've got a home page driven straight off the lot. In this chapter, I'll show you how you can customize it to fit your own particular needs and wants. You can modify your standard home page into your own customized vehicle.

Now it's time to learn how to use some of these advanced HTML concepts to tailor your home page to your needs. This chapter introduces you to a potpourri of neat things you can do with your home page. I cover a diverse set of topics, none too complicated to start using immediately.

Specifically, in this chapter, I show you how to:

- Split your single home page into a small set of integrated WWW pages

- Track how many visitors stop by and visit your home page

- Link to other Internet information such as FTP, UseNet, and Gopher

- Let visitors send you e-mail directly from Netscape

Expanding Your Home Page into a Home Site

When you graduated from college, you probably moved into a small single-room apartment—one where you could afford to pay the rent and utilities. You didn't have much furniture or decorations to arrange on the walls, but sooner or later, you realized that you needed to move to a larger apartment, and eventually to a house.

Just as your first apartment always got messy and cluttered, eventually, you will have too much information to fit on a single page. While a basic home page might serve most of your needs, once you start adding all of your personal and professional interests, toss in several images and multimedia clips, and create links to WWW pages all over the Internet, you may notice that your home page has become large and unwieldy. That's when it's time to expand your horizons and change your home page into a home site.

You'll still have a home page—that's the main starting point for visitors looking for information about you—but now your home page is linked to several other HTML documents pertaining to you. Combined together, I call this set of HTML documents your home site.

Expanding your home page into different Web pages is common as your knowledge of HTML matures. For example, as you may have noticed, my home page had a lot of different pieces of information that I was trying to fit on one page. Eventually, I was at the maximum limit with what would logically fit onto a single page, and I still had more information to add. So, I split it up into 8 different Web pages, all linked back and forth from my original page. Thus, you've created your own mini-Web of HTML documents.

Why Split Up Your Home Page

There are two important reasons for splitting your home page into a home site. The first is that it makes it easier for visitors to get the information that they want. If a potential employer stops by your home page, they don't really want to spend several minutes downloading text and images of your family; they want to see your resume and work experience. Making all of these aspects separate documents, they can choose to see only the information they really want. This adds more control to your visitors.

IV

Home Page Publishing

The second, and more selfish reason (it was my reason for splitting), is so you can add more spiffy graphics and personal information. My home page was already overburdened with graphics and multimedia files. Adding more would have made it practically unreadable for most WWW visitors. When I split my pages up, I was able to double the amount of graphics and neat images I could use. Practically every page has a graphic or multimedia file of some sort.

Design Your Home Site Correctly

Before you split up your home page, you've got to come up with a plan. Remember way back in chapter 2, where I talked about designing your single page appearance? This is the same process, except you're deciding the structure of your site and how your pages will link together.

Below, I've sketched out four possible ways you can choose to link your documents together. Each of these methods have their advantages and disadvantages in certain situations. You can choose whichever one works best for your home page.

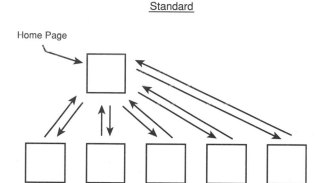

Standard—In this format, your home page links to each of the other documents in your home site, and documents all link directly back to your home page. This is the easiest and most common way to create a Web site.

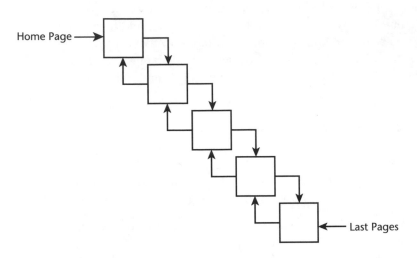

Waterfall—Your documents are linked in a predefined order so that there is only one path through all of your pages. Water can only flow in one direction, and so can your visitors.

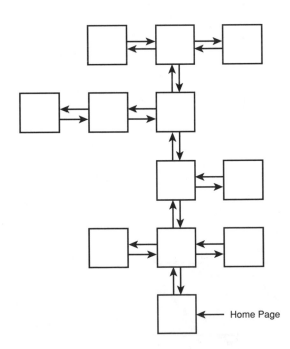

Skyscraper—To get to room 2676 in the Empire State Building, you've got to board the elevator and choose the 26th floor before you can walk down the hall to your location. In the Skyscraper model, some of your pages can only be read if visitors follow the right path.

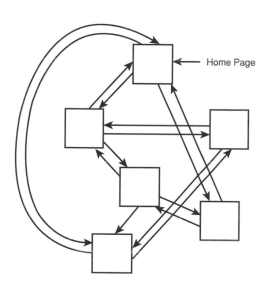

Web

Web—All of the pages in your site are linked to one another, allowing you to visit virtually any single page from another. This method is confusing when it gets out of hand, but is popular when your document links are used with moderation.

Note

Incidentally, in my home site, I use a hybrid of the methods above. If you combine the Standard and Web methods, you can see how my home site is organized. While you can reach all of the pages directly through my home page, several of my documents reference and link to each other as well.

Splitting Your Page

Once you've decided on a home site structure, it's time to actually split your pages. Using Hotdog, you can choose **File**, **Save As** from the menu bar and create new HTML files.

Try to give your files descriptive names so it's easier to make changes in the future. Having files named Page1.HTM, Page2.HTM, Page3.HTM, and so on aren't nearly as useful as academic.htm, personal.htm, and publish.htm.

> **Note**
>
> UNIX, Macintosh, and Windows 95 operating systems all support extended filenames. For example, now that I'm using Windows 95, I could name my three files **Academic Information.HTML, Personal Information.HTML,** and **Published Books.HTML.**

Make sure you add the <HTML>, <HEAD>, and <BODY> tags to each new page, as well as a new <TITLE> for the document. You have to go through the same motions as you did when you originally created your home page.

Each Web page that you create should not assume that the visitor came directly from your home page. Your separate Web pages can be linked from other sites. Each Web page should be self contained, and not missing important information (like your name) that people who linked to it might want to know.

Also, each of your Web pages should have a standard footer at the bottom that tells visitors who created the Web page, when it was last updated, and who to contact for more information. Just because you include that information on your home page doesn't mean you shouldn't bother with it on your other pages as well. In addition, it is also a good idea to include a link back to your home page to make navigating your site easier. Here's my footer in HTML:

```
<A HREF="http://www.cis.ohio-state.edu/~shafran">Andy Shafran's
Homepage</A><P>

<I> Last Updated July 28, 1995 by

<A HREF="mailto:shafran@cis.ohio-state.edu">Andy Shafran</A><BR>

shafran@cis.ohio-state.edu<I>
```

Figure 8.1 shows how the footer looks in one of my pages.

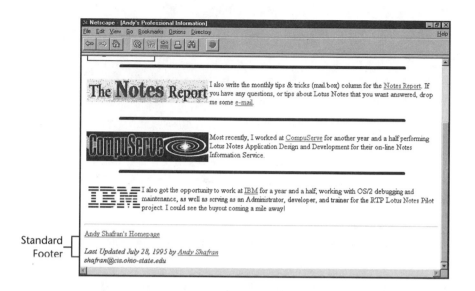

IV

Home Page Publishing

Fig. 8.1
It's a standard
footer that does
the trick nicely.

Standard
Footer

Tip

Don't forget to remove your HTML targets. When you're splitting your pages into smaller, easier chunks to read, targets are usually no longer necessary because each section is now a separate file.

Linking Your Pages Together

With your pages split, it's time to link your home page to each one of them. Make sure you link your pages together in an order that would make sense to anyone who would visit your home page.

For example, I have an online resumé page and one detailing my academic information. I could have linked my academic information Web page to my resumé (under education) instead of directly to my home page. Even though this makes sense logically, most visitors would never even know you had academic information available unless they looked at your resumé first. I chose to make it a link directly on my home page (with another link to it on my resumé as well).

You have several different options for linking your home site together. Personally, I use an unordered list on my page to depict each selection that visitors can choose, but you can use a table, or regular text just as successfully.

Here's my unordered list:

```
<UL>

<LI> Want to see my <A HREF="personal.html"> personal
information</A>?

<LI> You can also read about my <A
HREF="professional.html">professional information. </A>

<LI> WWW Documents relevant detailing my <A
HREF="classes.html">Academic information</A> and career at Ohio
State

<LI> As a full time writer (more or less), I have several published
<A HREF="pub/publish.html"> publications</A> for Que and The Notes
Report

<LI> I have several useful <A HREF="links.html">links</A> that I
use often.  They cover Web page creation, Broadway Musicals, and
much more

</UL>
```

Note

Notice how most of my HTML documents are located in the same directory as my original file. You can organize your HTML files into whichever directory structure you choose. I have a separate PUB directory because there are lots of images on that page that I wanted to keep together.

See figure 8.2 for how my home page looks now that it's linked to separate files.

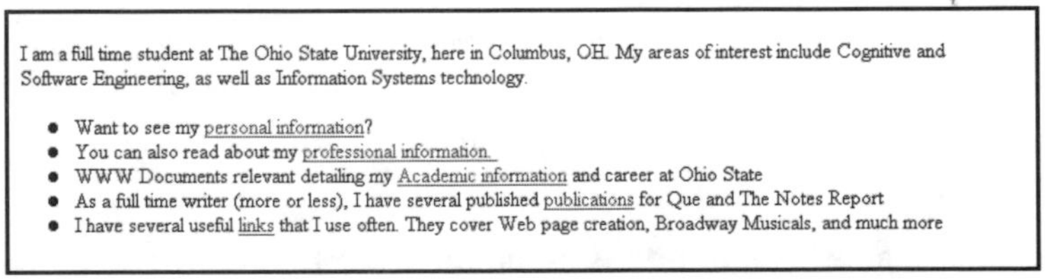

Fig. 8.2
The links look the same as they did when all of my information was in the same file.

I am a full time student at The Ohio State University, here in Columbus, OH. My areas of interest include Cognitive and Software Engineering, as well as Information Systems technology.

- Want to see my personal information?
- You can also read about my professional information.
- WWW Documents relevant detailing my Academic information and career at Ohio State
- As a full time writer (more or less), I have several published publications for Que and The Notes Report
- I have several useful links that I use often. They cover Web page creation, Broadway Musicals, and much more

Tracking How Many People Visit Your Home Page

One of the most popular requests for new home page owners is the ability to figure out how many people stop by their page. Without this information, you won't know if your home page is as popular as a Manhattan night club, or as barren as the Sahara desert. If you run your own Web server, or have an unusually friendly Web provider, you may be able to get that information just by asking them. The Web server software can automatically track such usage statistics.

In most cases, you've got to track your visitors yourself. There are several different ways to add an incremental counter to your home page. These counters keep track of every time someone visits your page and adds that increasing number to your home page.

First, I'll describe a simple counter that anyone on the WWW can use and add to their home page in under five minutes. Then I'll talk about some advanced options you have if you're really serious about keeping track of your home page visitors.

Adding the Simple Counter

While browsing the Web one day, I found a simple site that lets anyone who has a home page add an incremental counter to their page(s) by just adding a simple HTML link (like the kind you created in chapter 6). Nothing fancy, this counter requires no time consuming support, or special knowledge of advanced HTML code.

Once you insert a link to the counter onto your home page, the counter increments by one every time a visitor stops by. You link your home page to a database that counts your home page visitors.

You can put this counter on your home page by adding the following HTML to your document:

```
Number of visitors to this page:

<A HREF="http://www.forsmark.uu.se/counter.html"><IMG SRC="http://
www.forsmark.uu.se/cgi-bin/counter/YOUR-NAME-HERE" ALIGN=MIDDLE></A>
```

> **Note**
>
> Forsmark is a small technical college located in Germany that made this counter publicly available to anybody and everybody on the WWW.

All you have to do is replace the above text **YOUR-NAME-HERE** with your own name, and voila, you've got an incremental counter on your home page. Look at figure 8.3 to see what this easy-to-use counter looks like.

Fig. 8.3
Not a whopping number of visitors, but I've just started keeping count.

Counter —

> **Tip**
>
> You should place this link towards the bottom of your document. Netscape loads your home page from the top down, and it takes several additional seconds to link to the counter page and return with the current visitor number. Placing it on the bottom of your page makes it easier for visitors to ignore that short wait, because they can see the rest of your page.

> **Note**
>
> Businesses that are looking for a counter should read the following section. This simple counter is ideal only for home pages (businesses can have their Web provider add a counter, or make their own with a small charge). This will keep the free counter site from getting overloaded.

More Advanced Counters

There are several other, more advanced counter programs available for free on the WWW. The advantage of these other counter programs is that they work locally, on your own Web server. Visitors don't have to wait for Netscape to link to a counter halfway across the world before they can display the number of visits your page has had. If you expect your Web page to get lots of visits (more than 25 a day), it's probably in your best interest to look into using a different counter than the one above for these performance reasons.

Unfortunately, the other types of counters aren't nearly as easy to install as the counter I listed above. You must be familiar with computer programming, have advanced knowledge of HTML, and know a little on how a Web server works to use them properly. Below, I've listed several popular counter programs available for free. Each of the counters comes with instructions, and you should contact your Web provider with any installation questions (that's what you're paying them for).

- **http://www-mae.engr.ucf.edu/~ssd/counter.html**
  Here is the actual program of the counter used above, available for you to download and install at your own site.

- **http://purgatory.ecn.purdue.edu:20002/JBC/david/how.html**
  A step-by-step tutorial on adding counters to your Web page.

- **http://melmac.corp.harris.com/access_counts.html**
  Add a counter to your Web Server here.

Linking to Other Internet Resources

When I was writing this book, I needed to stay in constant communication with Que, my publisher. I was on the phone with them daily and regularly exchanged e-mail messages as well. When simple words weren't enough, I would fax information to them immediately, while other times, Federal Express became an important crutch. All these types of communication were part of a normal day.

The Internet works in a similar way, only on a much bigger scale. Thousands of computers need to constantly talk to each other and exchange information. Using various communication standards, or Internet protocols, computers communicate with each other in several different ways. Each of these different protocols have their own special uses, features and advantages. I wouldn't use a fax machine to transmit a 100 page manuscript, and likewise, I wouldn't try to e-mail a huge file to my publisher—there are better, more efficient methods of sending that information.

In chapter 6, I introduced links and showed you how to connect two HTML documents together using the HTTP Protocol. The HTTP Protocol was developed specifically for the World Wide Web, and was the first type of Internet communication that browsers, such as Netscape, supported.

Since then, several other popular Internet protocols are now supported and can be integrated into your home page. They work the same way as the links

I talked about in chapter 6, only you need to know the correct URL to use the various Internet protocols.

In this section, I show you how to use Hotdog to add HTML links to integrate FTP, Mailto, Gopher, and UseNet protocols into your home page.

Using Hotdog to Add Internet URLs

It's easy to link your home page to other Internet services with Hotdog. Click on the **Internet icon** in the Hotdog menu bar to bring up the create HyperText Link dialog box seen in figure 8.4.

Fig. 8.4
Hotdog lists all the possible link types you can create.

Choose the type of link you want to create, and Hotdog will prompt you for the full address of the site you want to link into. Figure 8.5 shows the choose newsgroup dialog box that appears when you click on **Go to a UseNet Newsgroup**.

Fig. 8.5
Hotdog adds a graphical interface to building your links.

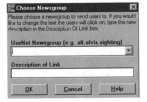

I recommend using Hotdog to build your Internet links. All you have to type is the link address and the text description you want to make hot, and Hotdog builds the link for you. Below, I've described how to add several of the most popular types of Internet links to your home page.

FTP

There are millions of different files available on the Internet. Everything from the latest shareware games to catalogs of recipes can be downloaded directly to your home computer using FTP (File Transfer Protocol).

Files that are accessible via FTP can be added directly to your home page. This convenience allows visitors the ability to download files without loading a separate FTP program. To add an FTP link, choose **Go to an FTP Server** from the Create HyperText Link dialog box.

Here's the FTP URL of Hotdog, the Web editor used in this book:

FTP Protocol Specified —ftp://ftp.sausage.com/pub/hdgsetup.exe——file to be downloaded   sub-directory the file is in
└——Internet domain address

Here's how I added that address to my home page:

```
<A HREF=ftp://ftp.sausage.com/pub/hdgsetup.exe > Download the
Hotdog Web Editor </A>
```

See, it's just like linking using the HTTP protocol, only with a different URL. In Netscape, **download the Hotdog Web editor** appears like any other link on your home page. When visitors click on that link, Netscape automatically opens up an FTP connection and downloads the specified file. See figure 8.6 for the window that appears in Netscape when I click on the FTP link.

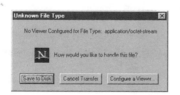

Fig. 8.6
Choose Save to Disk to save the FTPed file to your hard drive.

Note

The method I've described above works only for Anonymous FTP access. Anonymous FTP access allows anyone on the Internet to connect to a certain site and download files. Most FTP sites allow anonymous access.

However, there may be times where you want to connect to a password protected FTP site. If Hotdog required a password to download the editor, your FTP URL would look like this:

ftp://userid:password@ftp.sausage.com/pub/hdgsetup.exe

(continues)

(continued)

You must specify the user ID and password (listed in boldface above) when using a passworded FTP site.

Be careful when adding password protected FTP sites to your home page. Anyone who clicks on the link will be able to visit that FTP site using your user ID and password. Links to non-anonymous FTP sites are best used for Web pages no one else will ever see.

News

On the Internet, thousands of UseNet newsgroups exist, covering every topic imaginable. Whether you want to talk about Bruce Springsteen or Windows 95, there's bound to be a newsgroup for you.

You can link your home page to as many different newsgroups as you'd like just by knowing the full newsgroup name. To add a newsgroup link to your home page, choose **Go to a UseNet Newsgroup** from the Create HyperText Link dialog box. Heres the URL to the newsgroup where new Web pages and tools are announced:

Usenet News Protocol ——— **news:comp.infosystems.www.announce** ——— Newsgroup to read

To add this as a link to your home page, type the following HTML:

> **<LI><AHREF="news:comp.infosystems.www.announce">USENET Newsgroup:Comp.Infosystems.WWW.Announce</A>**

After clicking on the newsgroup link, Netscape brings up a list of available articles (see fig. 8.7) that you can choose from. Click on a message subject to read that particular newsgroup message.

Tip

Getting newsgroups to work properly with Netscape takes a bit of customization. To set Netscape properly, choose **Options**, **Preferences** from the Netscape menu bar. Then click on the tab labeled **Mail and News** as shown in figure 8.8. At the bottom of the screen, you can customize where Netscape retrieves newsgroup information from, and change the default number of articles that are shown. Click on the **OK** button to save your changes.

Fig. 8.7
This high volume newsgroup always has new messages to read.

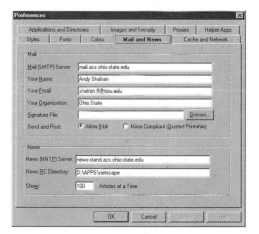

Fig. 8.8
Set your Netscape news options correctly if you start using links to newsgroups on your home page.

Note

Not only can you link your home page to a specific newsgroup, but you can also link to a specific message as well. For example, a message that I might post could be linked directly to my home page via the following URL:

    ashaf4$jir@osu.edu

However, due to the high volume of newsgroups, I don't recommend linking to a specific message. Within a few days, your link will probably expire because the message will be purged to make room for new ones.

Gopher

Another popular Internet application is Gopher. Developed at the University of Minnesota (hence the name), Gopher is a text-based menu system that allows Internet sites to sort and organize vast quantities of information. You must step through various levels of menus to find the information you want at a Gopher site.

Most Internet sites have Gopher menu systems, but they are increasingly less popular as more information migrates over to the WWW. Gopher is text only and not nearly as exciting to look at as a colorful Web page. Regardless, there is still a lot of information and activity using Gopher, and you may want to link some of that information to your home page. To include a Gopher link to your home page, choose **Go to a Gopher** from the Create HyperText Link dialog box.

Here's a sample Gopher URL that links you to the U.S. State Department Travel Advisory on France.

Gopher Protocol specification   complete path to the gopher file

Internet address of gopher information

gopher://gopher.stolaf.edu:70/00/Internet%20Resources/US State-Department-Travel-Advisories/Current-Advisories/france

Below is the HTML code used when I added that link to my home page. Figure 8.9 shows how the Gopher page appears in Netscape.

```
<A HREF="gopher://gopher.stolaf.edu:70/00/
Internet%20Resources/US-State-Department-Travel-Advisories/
Current-Advisories/france">Gopher report on the US Travel
Advisory on France</A>
```

Fig. 8.9
Gopher may not be as pretty as the WWW, but still has a lot of current information.

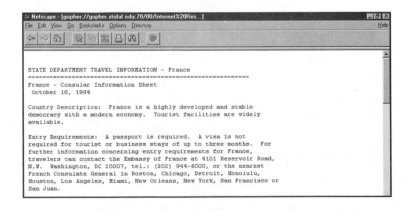

> **Note**
>
> Did you notice the %20 in the Gopher URL above? WWW browsers don't know how to interpret spaces in their HTML links. You can get around that by replacing spaces with the text: **%20**. Netscape knows how to read and translate that special code automatically.
>
> If by chance you need to add an actual % into your URL, replace it with the **%25** code.

E-mail

E-mail, or electronic mail, is the most popular way to communicate privately between users on the Internet. Usually, users must load a separate program to send e-mail across the Internet. But with Netscape, you can embed e-mail addresses directly into your home page and send e-mail with a single click.

Most Web page designers add an e-mail link to themselves at the bottom of their page so that visitors can easily send them questions or comments without switching back to their separate e-mail program. To include an e-mail link to your home page, choose **Let the User Send Mail to Someone** from the Create HyperText Link dialog box.

On my home page, I have an e-mail link to myself on every page. Here's my URL:

E-mail protocol specification ────────────────── Internet e-mail address
Mailto:shafran@cis.ohio-state.edu

This URL tells Netscape to bring up a blank e-mail message and address it to **shafran@cis.ohio-state.edu** (as shown in figure 8.10). My HTML code appears below:

<A HREF="mailto:shafran@cis.ohio-state.edu">E-mail to Andy Shafran</A>

> **Caution**
>
> Not all Netscape users have their e-mail configured properly. To configure your Netscape browser to send e-mail, choose **Options**, **Preferences** from the Netscape menu bar and click on the **Mail and News** tab. Make sure your mail server (the first box) is set properly.

Fig. 8.10
E-mail capabilities
to your home page
is a welcome
addition.

Part V

Adding the Final Touches to Your Web Page

list of WWW Links

y keeps their own list of "cool" links. This is my list of links that I actually use and reference.

Links
ntice Hall Publishing
cmillan Publishing
Davis Net
On-Line
rdwatch Magazine
de Magazine
es Links
s SmartNotes Magazine
s Notes Resources
s on the Web
upware Links
labra Share
wing neat HTML features & Pages
cam (integrated movement on pages for Netscape 1.1)
Time Audio
Audio Home Page
ryware Development Corporation

List Element

en to set up lists. The individual list item
in, and Numbered Lists are defined with
ns in Definition lists are defined with <DT
<dd> for the definition. For bulleted lists,
the browser's default bullets with your ov
lling in the Use Image field.

You say what, we say how.

Choose how you want your materials
delivered by clicking on the method below

SponsorNet

☒Yahoo ☒Starting Point ☒WebCrawler ☒EINet Galaxy ☒Lycos ☒Harvest ☒What's New Toc
☒Infoseek ☒Whole Internet Catalog ☒Open Text Web Index ☒World Wide Web Worm ☒Apol

☐JumpStation ☐New Rider's WWW Yellow Pages ☐TheYellowPages.com ☐Netcenter ☐NIKOS

Title:

URL:
http://

Category:
Health & Fitness   If Other, please Specify

Start | Micro... | Nets... | Netsca... | Explor... | HotDo... | Corrine... | WinQV... | telnet -

The Elephant Page in Barney's Circus

There are over 25 elephants that make up the mammoth creature ent
Barney's circus. We have elephants from all over the world, includin
extremely rare albino elephant. You won't want to miss any of these
creatures here at Barney's Circus.

- The Albino Elephant (63K)
- African Elephants (32K)
- More Elephant Pictures
- Watch the elephant performance (video - 3 meg)
- Buy an elephant ride today!

Other Ele

- The ele   Zoo
- Nationa   avannah
- Elepha

Unknown File Type

No Viewer Configured for File Type: application/oc

How would you like to handle this file?

Save to Disk   Cancel Transfer   Configure a

Welcome to Andy's Home

All visitors are welcome!

Thanks for stopping by my web page. It is an ongoing project and will probably not be finished until Chapter 10 of
am getting ready to graduate from The Ohio State University and hope to pursue a full time job writing, creating
or performing Lotus Notes consulting services. I'll probably just end up being a bum!

Compact List
Multi-column
Internet

Chapter 9

Forms, Clickable Images, and Beyond

This is the chapter where you learn how to add some heavy-duty HTML features to your home page. Clickable image maps, forms, and CGI Usage are all important buzz words and phrases that you'll learn how to use in this chapter.

Forms and clickable image maps are two of the hottest parts of the WWW because they allow an unprecedented amount of interactivity between Web surfers and the pages they visit. Clickable image maps allow visitors to click on various parts of images included on the page to link to different Web pages. Forms let visitors fill out screens of information and interactively exchange them between Netscape and Web sites.

Besides learning about forms and clickable maps, you'll also take a whirlwind tour of the latest web advances coming down the road. New technologies are constantly being released and integrated into the WWW. You should be familiar with these new features so you can recognize them while browsing the Web, and add them to your home page soon.

Specifically, in this chapter you learn how to:

- Specify an image to be used as a clickable image map
- Add a simple clickable map on your home page
- Create a basic form on your home page
- Recognize new WWW technologies with HTML 3.0

Understanding the Common Gateway Interface (CGI)

Before I can talk about clickable maps and forms, you first need to understand the WWW Common Gateway Interface (CGI). Specifically, CGI allows you to create programs (often called CGI scripts) to supply information from other sources into your home page. For example, if you were a real estate agent, you could write a CGI program that searches through a database of available listings and returns houses that are appropriate for your buyers.

I like to think of CGI as the customs officials you encounter when traveling to another country. CGI makes sure that all the information traveling between your home page and other data sources flows correctly and is displayed in the correct format.

CGI scripts are actual programs that are written in UNIX script language, C, Perl, Applescript, Visual Basic, or virtually any programming language you are familiar with, as long as it'll run on your Web server. In this chapter, I introduce you to a couple of basic CGI scripts, one for image maps, and the other for adding a form to your home page (both written in UNIX scripting language). This is just the tip of the iceberg. With CGI scripts you could create huge programs that run when triggered by your home page. For more information on using advanced CGI features in your home page, see Que's *Using HTML, Special Edition* by Tom Savola.

What Is an Image Map?

In chapter 5, you learned how to use Hotdog to add basic images, icons, and graphics to your home page. These images made your home page attractive to look at and fun to use. In the next chapter, you learn how to link those images to other HTML files.

Image maps are related to standard images, with one major difference. When you link a regular image to another HTML file, it doesn't matter where the image is clicked; the same document always appears. Image maps are different. With an image map, you can link various parts of the image to different HTML files.

There are several good uses for image maps. For example, Italy might place a virtual map online. Using your mouse, you'd click on whichever region or city of Italy you wanted to learn more about. Clicking on Rome might bring up the Coliseum, and Pisa could link to that famous leaning tower. Or Boeing might place a picture of its new 777 plane on the WWW. Visitors could click on different parts of the cockpit to learn how the plane operates.

Take a look at figure 9.1 for a better understanding of what I mean. In this figure, I have three different shapes combined together. A standard image would link to the same file, no matter where on the image you clicked. I can tell Netscape to bring up a different file depending on which shape is clicked on.

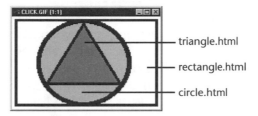

Fig. 9.1
These images—the triangle, rectangle and circle—are clickable.

Virtually any image can become an image map—and they're easy to create. With the right tools (and they're provided for you on the home page CD), anyone can add an image map to their home page in ten minutes.

> **Caution**
>
> Adding a clickable image map to your home page requires special permissions set by your Web server. Your Web server must allow and support CGI scripts. Most Web servers automatically support them, but it's always a good idea to ask your Web provider—just in case. Without having CGI script server support, your clickable map will never work.
>
> My Web server, for example, doesn't support scripts, so you won't be able to stop by home page for a live demonstration.

Creating Clickable Image Maps

Anyone can add an image map to their home page in just a few minutes. There's no complicated programming, new HTML tags to learn, or difficult WWW concepts to understand. I'll step you through a real-life example, creating an image map just how I would for my home page (if my Web provider could support image maps).

There are really only three steps in creating an image map.

1. First you've got to find a good image to use.

2. Then, you define which parts of the image link to which HTML documents using special image map software.

3. Finally, you tell your home page and Web server about the image map and install the necessary files.

Getting the Right Image

The first (and most difficult) step in creating an image map is finding the right image to use. Practically any type of picture, icon, or graphic can be an effective image map, but some make better choices than others. As a general rule of thumb, you should tend to use images that are easy to delineate and separate into different sections. Images where everything blends together are sometimes hard to use because visitors can't tell the difference between the various clickable sections (Picasso paintings make terrible image maps).

For this example, I'm going to use a simple image that I created from scratch (shown in fig. 9.2). Once you've selected an image, you're ready to go on to the next step. This sample image is ideal because it's extremely easy to identify the different parts of the image and which HTML files they are linked to.

Fig. 9.2
By land, sea, or air, this clickable image lets you pick your preferred delivery method with your mouse.

Mapping the Image Coordinates

Once you've chosen your image, the next step is create a separate text file which tells your Web server how to interpret the clicks on various parts of the image. This file, called a mapfile, defines different areas on your image and tells your Web server which HTML document to link to when a certain area is clicked upon.

As you learned in chapter 5, when you set the height and width of images on your page, images are measured in pixels, or dots displayed on your screen. (A standard VGA monitor is 640 pixels wide and 480 pixels high.) In your mapfile, you must specify the different clickable areas by their pixel coordinates.

Tip

The pixel number system for every image begins at 0,0—which represents the upper left-hand corner of the image. Numbers steadily increase as you move right and down on the image.

Your first step is to decide which area of the image to link to which HTML files. It's just like drawing blueprints of your image (see fig. 9.3).

Fig. 9.3
Here's how I want the different clickable areas defined.

Once you've decided how to split up your image, it's time to actually create your textual mapfile. On the home page CD I've included several image map utilities that will create your MAP file automatically. My favorite is Map THIS!. Using Map THIS!, you can use your mouse to draw and link the different clickable areas of your image. You can find Map THIS! in the \HOMEPAGE\IMAGEMAP\MAPTHIS subdirectory on the CD-ROM.

Note

You can install Map THIS! onto your computer by copying it to your hard drive, or just run it directly from the home page CD.

Once you've started Map THIS!, choose **File**, **New** to bring up the Make New Image Map dialog box. Choose **lets go find one** to bring up a file box that searches your hard drive for GIF files (Map THIS! doesn't work with JPEG images). Find your GIF file and click on the **OK** button to bring up the image in Map THIS! as shown in figure 9.4.

Fig. 9.4

Here's my file ready to be made into an image map.

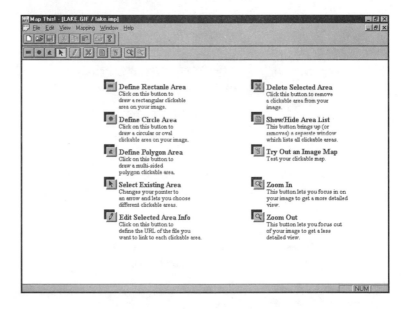

On your image, you can define several different clickable shapes including circles, squares, and polygons (see fig. 9.4). Using Map THIS!, you actually draw these shapes directly onto your image and link them to separate HTML files. Click on the icon of the shape you want to draw and then actually draw on your image. Each clickable area you define is surrounded by a very light dotted line, as shown in figure 9.5.

Fig. 9.5
I have three rectangle shapes defined on my sample image.

Once your shapes are drawn, you've got to tell Map THIS! the URL of the HTML file you want each piece to link to. Click on the **Select Existing Area** icon (the little arrow) and click on a clickable area. Now click on the **Edit Selected Area Info** icon (the pencil) to bring up the settings for that clickable region (see fig. 9.6).

Fig. 9.6
Notice the pixel coordinates in the top of this box.

Type in the URL of the HTML file you want to load. To load a file that is in the same directory as the page this image is on, you only need to type in the file name.

When you are finished, choose **File**, **Save** from the menu bar to bring up the **Info About This Mapfile dialog box** (see fig. 9.7).

V

Final Touches

Fig. 9.7

Type important info about your image map in this dialog box.

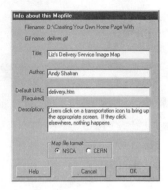

From here, type a description and title of the image map file. You can also type a default URL which brings up an HTML document when non-defined areas of the image are clicked upon. At the bottom, specify the type of server your Web provider is using, because different servers use different types of mapfiles.

Tip

Map THIS! recommends setting a default URL that appears when a non-clickable part of your image map is clicked on. I recommend setting it to your current HTML document (just type in the name of the file the image appears on) if you don't have another default document that appears.

Note

Different kinds of Web servers require different kinds of image map files. These files are essentially the same, only formatted slightly differently. Map THIS! allows you to save your image map in NSCA and CERN Web server format (the two most popular Web servers). Ask your Web provider if you arent sure what kind of image map format to use.

When you're finished, click on the **OK** button. You'll then be prompted for a file name (mine is named **delivery.imp**). Here's what my image map file in NSCA server format looks like for this example (with a lot of mumbo-jumbo added in by Map THIS!). The numbers at the bottom represent the actual pixels of each clickable area:

default delivery.htm
Links the image of the ship to the correct HTML file
rect ship.htm 0,169 159,320
Links the image of the truck to the correct HTML file
rect truck.html 164,169 314,320
Links the image of the plane to the correct HTML file
rect plane.html 319,168 475,320

Adding the Image to Your Home Page

All you've got left to do is add the image to your home page and link it to the image map file you just created. The only difference is that you need to add the ISMAP keyword to your <IMG> tag. This keyword tells Netscape to re-member where users clicked on the image and to send those pixel coordi-nates to your mapfile for interpretation.

Here's the HTML that I use to add the example we've just created:

```
<A HREF="cgi-bin/delivery.imp">

<IMG ISMAP SRC="images/delivery.gif">

</A>
```

Deciphered, the above HTML says: Place the image **delivery.gif** on-screen (in the images subdirectory) and mark it as an Image Map. Then link it to **delivery.imp** located in the **cgi-bin** sub-directory. Once you've added the necessary HTML to your home page, Netscape uses **delivery.imp** to inter-pret clicks on your image and bring up separate files.

Your clickable map appears like any other image on your home page.

Advanced CGI Usage

So far, I've introduced you to two popular ways that CGI scripting can be used on your home page—but that's just the tip of the iceberg. Since CGI scripts can be written in virtually any programming language, they offer a wide realm of flexibility for your home page.

Below, I've listed some other popular things you can do with CGI scripts and included URLs so you can check these sites out.

Interactive Chat	Have a conversation with other people logged on to the same web site directly through Netscape. **http://www.irsociety.com/webchat/ webchat.html**
Guest Book	Let visitors to your home page sign in your guestbook, so you have a record of who's stopped by for a visit. **http://128.172.69.106:8080/cgi-bin/ cgis.html**
Yahoo Programming Index	This is the best site to stop by to learn more about CGI Programming. **http://www.yahoo.com/ Computers_and_Internet/Internet/ World_Wide_Web/Programming/**

Chapter 10

Important Design Considerations

After reading the first nine chapters, you've made it through all the HTML tags, links, and images and created a decent looking home page. This section teaches you how to put the final touches on your home page before you make it available for millions of WWW surfers to see.

So far I've mentioned many different tips and tricks for creating a high quality Web page. Whether it's organizing your text with lists and tables, or linking your images properly, you've learned how important it is to properly present information on your home page.

This chapter helps you put all those tips together. I introduce several different design concepts and show you how they make your home page look better and easier to take care of. If your home page is the canvas, this chapter is the paint brush that you will use to create a masterpiece of a home page.

Specifically, in this chapter you learn how to:

- Make sure your home page has a consistent look to it

- Keep your home page current to attract repeat visitors

- Structure your HTML file so it is readable and maintainable in the future

- Add comments to your HTML file

- Validate your Web page with an automated HTML checker

Home Page Design Tips

As you've learned in this book, you can create a home page in just a matter of minutes. Hotdog helps you decipher complicated HTML tags with ease and lets you add new elements with your mouse. However, while creating a basic home page isn't too difficult, there are several things you should keep in mind when designing how your home page appears. In this section I'll go over a couple of popular (but simple) design tips that will help your home page look great.

Measure Your Page's Consistency

All telephones work the same. You pick up the receiver and start dialing the person you want to reach. When you're done, you hang up the receiver to stop your conversation. Sure, some phones require a special number to be dialed (like 9) to work, and others hide their buttons in hard-to-find spots, but all of them generally work the same. This consistency is what lets you know how to use a phone from anywhere in the world.

Visitors to your Web site appreciate that same type of consistency on your home page. All your Web pages should have a consistent style about them. Soon, visitors will know where to find that information on your Web pages without even looking.

Some examples of consistency are:

- Use the same headline format on every Web page. If you use the <H1> tag to label your home page, then you should use an <H1> tag to label every page in your site. Using different sized headlines on different pages will look odd.

- Add graphics and images in similar ways throughout your home page. If some of your graphics link to other Web sites, and others don't, visitors might not recognize which graphics are which and could get confused.

- Include the same information in the page's footer. At the bottom of every Web page you include important information about when it was created and who to contact for further information. Add this same default footer to every page in your site.

Brevity Is a Virtue

Some people like to compare the World Wide Web to a book that people can read and jump around from page to page. I prefer to liken the WWW to a glossy magazine—one where people flip through the pages randomly. Every now and then a story or headline might catch their eye, but for the most part, pages are being flipped about as fast as their hand can move. With a short reader attention span, magazines have to present their information in a short and usable nature.

With this in mind, it's a good idea to keep your Web page concise and to the point. Using a mouse, people browse through Web pages quickly. If something looks long and boring to read, they keep going until they see something that catches their eye. Think of your own browsing techniques. It's easy to run out of patience when browsing the WWW. If there is too much information, or something doesn't jump out and grab you, you're more likely to jump to another page before slowly reading and digesting several paragraphs of text. Figure 10.1 shows you what a home page looks like when it has too much text on it.

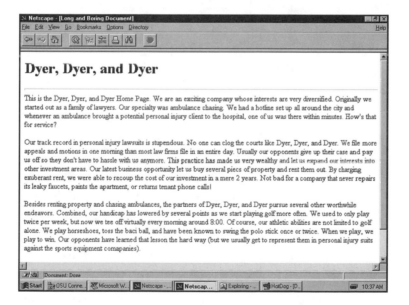

Fig. 10.1
Nobody will bother reading this; it's boring and long winded.

If you really have a lot of information to put on your home page, consider splitting the information up onto several different pages (see "Splitting Your Home Page into a Home Site" in chapter 8) and letting visitors link to the various pieces they want to read. This keeps them from becoming information overloaded.

To keep readers interested, and my home page brief, I use a simple rule of thumb that I call the three by three rule. Basically, the three by three rule tells me not to ever place more than three paragraphs (each with three sentences) together on a home page. After three paragraphs, readers become bored and move on. Instead, I use lists and tables to bring out important information and catch visitors' eyes.

> **Tip**
>
> Also keep in mind that every person that visits your home page must download everything that's on it (including all the text and pictures) before reading it. The smaller your page, the less people have to wait, twiddling their thumbs, for your home page to download. Remember that text downloads *much* faster than images. An entire page of text can download faster than a single image.

Don't Overdo Your Web Page with Glitz

Along the same lines as above, don't let your home page get out of hand with too much glamour and glitz. Everyone knows that you can add lots of pictures, sound clips, cool forms and clickable maps to your home page, just don't overuse these neat and impressive aspects of HTML.

When your home page uses so many different features all at once, it becomes difficult to read and hard to even look at. Don't try to add every neat HTML feature and trick you can think of to the same page. Although it's an impressive display of WWW knowledge and ability, it'll be gaudy to look at and impossible to understand.

Keep Your Home Page Alive

Every Thursday night, a new episode of *Seinfeld* comes on. Every week, when you turn the TV on, you know that you aren't going to see the same episode you watched last time because that would be boring. Except for the summer, new episodes are weekly occurrences. Can you imagine if there was only one episode, and NBC played it over and over again? You'd watch it the first time, and maybe see the rerun once, but after that, you'd switch channels. The reason you keep coming back Thursday at 9:00 is because you know you'll see something new.

You should practice this same philosophy on your home page. If you create a basic page and never update it or make changes, why would anyone come back? After one or two stops, they've seen everything there is to see on your home page and will start visiting other WWW spots instead.

The key to getting visitors to come back again and again is to constantly update it to keep information fresh and new. One great example of a constantly updating site is the Weather Channel's home page (**http:// www.infi.net/weather**) as shown in figure 10.2 below. Every time you visit, you can get current weather maps and information.

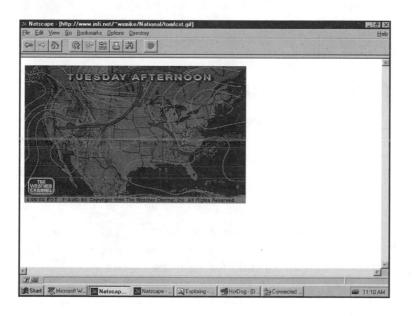

Fig. 10.2
Can you imagine if this page was never updated?

Once you've built a basic home page, keeping it fresh, new, and exciting is difficult, but well worth the trouble. For example, lawyers might keep a list of links relating to landmark precedents and decisions that their clients might be interested in. Accountants might note recent tax changes, and offer regular tips on how to prepare for April 15th. Remember Roxanne's home page (way back in chapter 2)? Well, she constantly updates it to include new information. Even though she doesn't offer forms, image maps, and multimedia files, I'll still stop by her page regularly. Figure 10.3 shows this week's tax topic.

Fig. 10.3
Roxanne knows how to get people to come back again—talk about money.

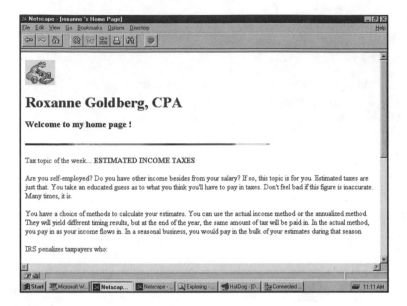

Improving Your HTML Code

One of the most common problems that I notice with Web pages most people never even notice. I'm referring to how the HTML text (called source files) appears when you look at it as a straight text document (in Hotdog, or any other text editor). Since Netscape reads HTML tags and formats based on tags, you usually never even see the underlying HTML file unless you've created it.

While technically it doesn't matter what your HTML source file looks like, you'll find that it makes a big difference when you try updating and making changes to your home page in the future. It doesn't take much time, or effort, to structure your HTML source file properly. You won't immediately reap many benefits from these few suggested improvements, but you'll be glad you did for future updates.

In six months, you may not remember why you used a table instead of a list to display your personal information, or spend six hours trying to decipher your cryptic HTML tags. That's why you should add comments to your home page. Comments never appear in Netscape, they only show up when you are reading your home page as a text file.

> **Note**
>
> In the world of computer programmers, these guidelines are strictly enforced as coding standards. That's because different people often work on the same program. So, everyone has to follow the same formatting standards, to make sure their work is readable. While no one else may be looking over your shoulder and grading your home page, following these guidelines is a must for formatting your HTML source code.

Make It Readable

The easiest thing you can do with your home page is to make it readable as a text file. There are only two exceptions to this general rule: tabs and returns. They don't affect the way the home page is laid out, the tags do that. Web browsers will ignore any and all tabs or returns. This means separating paragraphs of text, separating and making links easy to read, and lining up related information such as lists and tables.

Take a look at figures 10.4 and 10.5. Both of them look *exactly the same* when displayed with Netscape. In figure 10.4, the text is a confused, jumbled mess of text that is practically impossible to read. Just a simple use of tabs, returns, and spaces (shown in figure 10.5) cleans up that mess. Which would you rather work with?

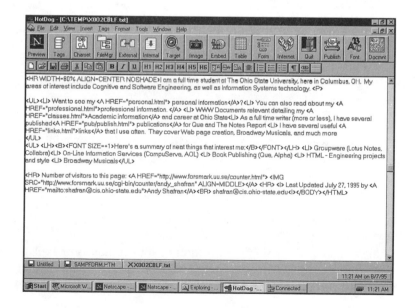

Fig. 10.4
HTML formatted like this is NOT fun, nor easy to work with.

Fig. 10.5
Try formatting
your home page's
HTML like this.
It's much easier to
take care of.

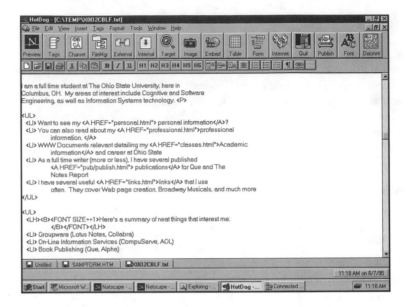

Your goal is to make your HTML file as readable as possible. Don't be afraid to use the tab or spacebar to line items up or separate paragraphs of text by hitting the enter key.

> **Tip**
>
> One popular way of formatting your source code is by typing your HTML tags in all CAPS. This makes the tags stand out and easier to notice when you quickly scan a document. Netscape isn't case sensitive, and doesn't care whether your <HMTL> tag looks like <html>, <Html>, or <hTmL>.

Comment your HTML

Another popular way to enhance your HTML source code is by adding comments. Comments are specially marked sentences and phrases that never appear in Netscape, but are part of the HTML source code. In your HTML source code, comments are surrounded by <!— and —>.

<!— Heres a sample comment —>

Comments are particularly useful for recording your thoughts or explaining complicated pieces of HTML code. For example, if you use an image map on your home page, you might want to include a comment that explains what choices the image map offers. Since you may not have the image handy when updating your source code later, this would be useful information to have available. See my example below:

<!— This image map lets people choose their delivery type.

    Truck   > truck.html

    Airplane   > airplane.html

    Ship   > ship.html

See the image or MAP file for more information. —>

<A HREF="delivery.imp">
<IMG SRC="delivery.gif">
</A>

Note

While Netscape is particularly good at reading comments in your source file, other browsers sometimes have trouble recognizing comments. If you want to make sure that your HTML source file is browser-proof, then follow these few rules when commenting your source code.

1. Don't use _____ inside of your comment; it may fool the browser that the comment is completed.

2. Place "<!—" and "—>" comments at the beginning and end of every line. Some browsers don't recognize comments that span multiple lines (why, I don't know).

3. Don't use other HTML tags inside of comments. This may cause other browsers to ignore the comment tags entirely.

Caution

Make sure you don't include private information in your home page comments because they can be read by anybody who visits your home page. Using the Netscape **View**, **Source** command, comments appear along with the rest of the source code. Passwords, personal phone numbers, and inappropriate language and remarks are examples of bad comment information.

Test Your Web Page

In college, before you submitted a term paper, you always gave it one final run through and look-see. You'd break out the spell checker and give it to friends to read before submitting it to your professor. Even though you spent a lot of time creating the perfect term paper, you almost invariably found small errors and silly mistakes that could cost you credit.

Can your Web page make the grade? Before you put your home page on the WWW and start announcing it to millions of people to visit (that's next chapter), you want to run a final look-see on your home page as well. With a fine tooth comb, you should check it over for common and easily preventable errors. This section shows you how to check your home page for common mistakes and validate it according to HTML standards.

Preview Your Page

Using Hotdog, you can preview your HTML document anytime you wish. All you've got to do is click on the **Preview** button located at the top of the Hotdog screen. Netscape loads up with the current HTML document automatically.

Give a good look to your home page. Here's a list of simple, but important things to check when looking at your home page, and how to fix the problems:

- **Make sure your paragraphs are split up properly**
  A common mistake is to forget the <P> tag between paragraphs. Without this tag, your paragraphs of text bunch together no matter how they appear in Hotdog. If your paragraphs are too far apart using the <P> tag, try using <BR> instead. This tag doesn't add an extra space between paragraphs.

- **Ensure that images appear where they should**
  When you start adding images to your home page, it is easy to use the wrong keywords (accidentally aligning an image on the right side of the screen instead of the left). Make sure your image is properly placed and sized on your home page and that text flows around the image correctly.

- **All of your HTML tags are closed**
  A very common problem with home pages is forgetting or not closing a tag properly. In my home page shown in figure 9.6, I forgot to add the / to the </H1> closing tag at the top of my page. Oops, that one little

mistake made quite a difference. Fortunately, you'll be using Hotdog to add most of your tags, but you might change a tag accidentally.

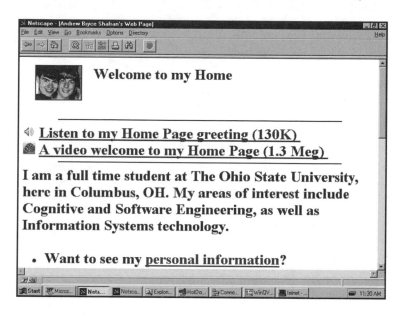

Fig. 10.6
This page is not for people who have bad eyesight, it's just a simple typo.

■ **All of your links work correctly**
If you are going to include HyperText links on your home page, make sure they work right, otherwise visitors see a screen that looks like figure 10.7. A common mistake, mistyping URLs is easily avoided. Several tools exist that automatically check all of the links included in your home page. Try using the MOMSpider (**http://www.ics.uci.edu/ WebSoft/MOMspider/**) or Checker (**http://www.ugrad.cs. ubc.ca/spider/q7f192/branch/checker.html**) to do this automatically.

■ **Spell check your page**
Spell checking your page is probably one of the easiest and most effective ways of improving your page's appearance. Misspelled words signify that you didn't take the time necessary to check out your page. If you purchase Hotdog Pro, you get a high-quality built in spell checker. I just copy and paste text from Netscape into Microsoft Word and run the Word Spell Checker from there. It is cost effective that way.

Use Another Browser

Although this book is geared for optimizing your home page for Netscape visitors, it's a good idea to check it out using another popular browser or two.

V

Final Touches

Your home page may look fantastic in Netscape, but impossible to read for Mosaic users. You want it to be read by anyone on the WWW.

Fig. 10.7
Web Surfers hate to see this screen, it means a link has been broken.

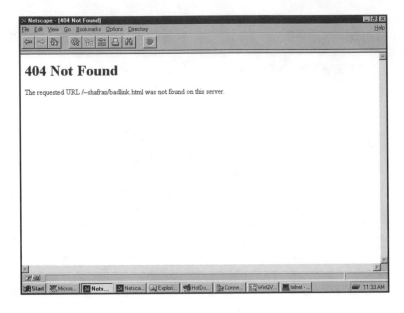

While youre not worried about taking advantage of all the advanced Netscape features, you want your home page to be readable for anyone who visits. Figure 10.8 shows my home page in Mosaic 2.0.

Fig. 10.8
Mosaic displays my home page almost as well as Netscape.

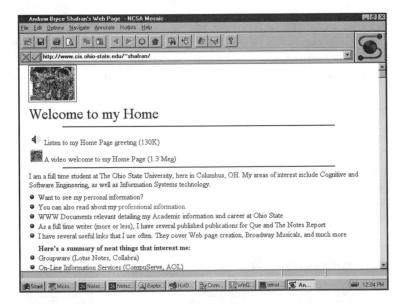

> **Tip**
>
> Older browsers typically don't support all of the new HTML and Netscape extensions. They may display items such as tables in a jumbled fashion. For example, older versions of Mosaic don't recognize tables, but 2.0 (the current version) does. Make sure you are always using the newest version of a WWW browser for this reason.

Test and Validate Your HTML Document

After you've run through your HTML code with the simple checklist above, you might think your home page is spotless and in ship-shape condition. However, it's also worth your time running an HTML Validation Tool (created by the World Wide Web Consortium) over your home page. These tools look at your HTML source code and evaluate according to the official definition of how HTML should be used. Since HTML is a world-wide standard there is a very strict definition of how it is to be used called a DTD (Document Type Definition)—it's the Websters Dictionary of the HTML world. You can take a look at the official HTML standards at:

**http://www.w3.org/hypertext/WWW/MarkUp/html-spec/
html-pubtext.html**.

> **Note**
>
> Netscape's extensions work is above and beyond the official HTML definition, but don't interfere with the official definition. Stop by the Netscape home page **(http://www.netscape.com)** for official definition information on their extensions.

The validation tools don't care what your home page looks like, how many links or graphics you include, or whether your paragraphs of information make sense. They only care whether or not you properly use HTML tags.

HTML validation tools are important because they ensure that your home page will be able to be read by browsers and cool WWW enhancements in the future.

For example, most browsers will interpret your HTML to the best of their ability. So, if you forgot to add the <HTML> and </HTML> tags to your home page, Netscape recognizes other HTML tell-tale signs and displays your document properly. A validation tool would recognize that you forgot the <HTML> tags and give you a reminder that your home page isn't official until it contains that tag.

In the future, other WWW tools might become available and not recognize your home page if it doesn't meet official HTML standards. So while an HTML validator may not improve the way your home page looks, it's an important tool for future compatibility.

HTML Validator

Let's check your home page with the easiest to use and most popular HTML validation service located at **http://www.halsoft.com/html-val-svc/** as shown in figure 10.9. You tell the HAL Validation Service the URL of the document you want it to check, and it will link there automatically. Within a few moments, you'll know whether or not your home page meets HTML standards, and if not, what you can do to fix it.

Fig. 10.9
The HAL Validation Service checks to see if you have written a technically correct home page.

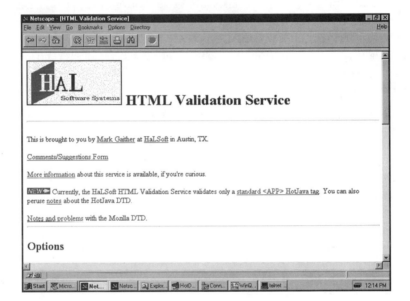

Note

To validate your home page, it must first be available on the WWW, not your personal computer. The Hal Validation Service cannot evaluate HTML files on your local computer because it requires a valid URL to work properly.

The first step in validating your home page is selecting the level of HTML you want to use. The HAL Validation Service allows you to test four different levels of HTML: Level 2 (the current standard), Level 3 (forthcoming standard), Mozilla (the nickname for the Netscape extensions), and HotJava compatibility (Java is the advanced language I talked about in chapter 9 and HotJava is the browser used to view it).

Since this book describes using all sorts of Netscape enhancements to make your page look better, choose **Mozilla**. Then, in the **Check Documents by URL box**, type in your home page's URL. Then click on the **submit URLs for validation button** to validate your home page. Figure 10.10 shows my Netscape screen *before* I try to validate my home page.

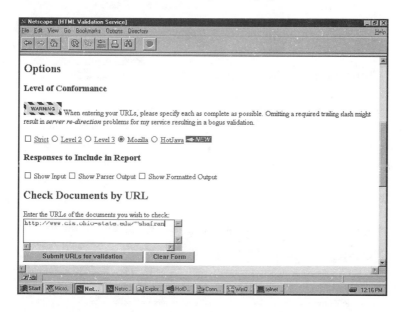

Fig. 10.10
I'm getting ready to validate my home page.

After clicking the button, the validation service fetches your home page and tests it for a variety of HTML faults and problems. If your home page fails the validation service, a screen appears that informs you why you have failed and helps you diagnose the problem. Once your home page passes the validation tests, figure 10.11 appears.

Fig. 10.11
Hooray, my home
page is valid!

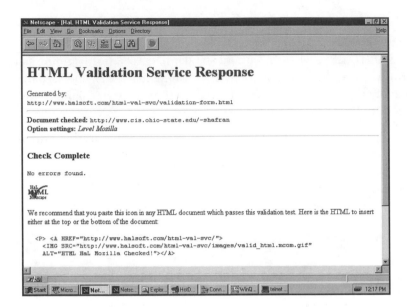

You can now add the HTML checked image to your home page if you wish.
The HAL Validation Service even gives you the HTML you want to add to
your home page. All you have to do is highlight the text and choose **Edit**,
Copy from the menu bar, and **Edit**, **Paste** into your home page in Hotdog.
I proudly display the validation icon at the bottom of my home page (see fig.
10.12).

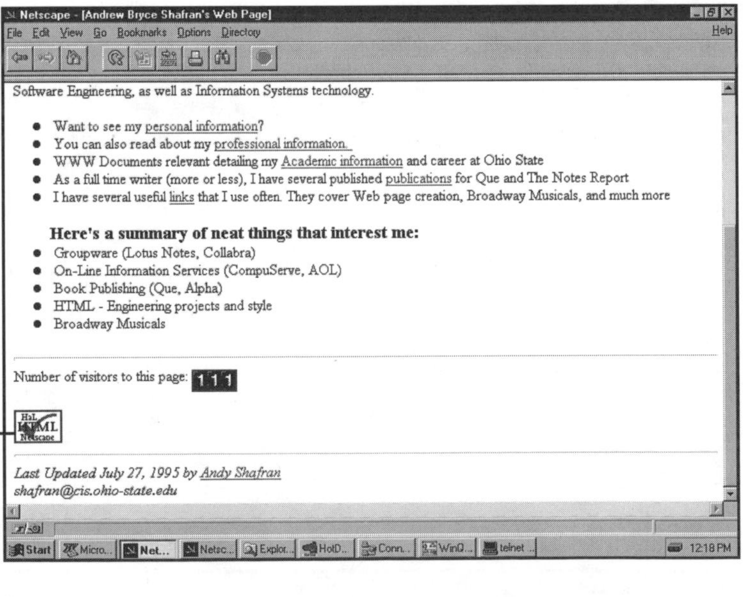

Fig. 10.12
This lets other
people know that I
write good HTML.

The validation
icon on my
home page

Other Validation Tools

Besides the HAL Validation Service, several other tools exist that let you check your home page according to HTML specifications. Below, I've listed some of the more popular HTML checking programs, and given their URLs.

- Weblint: (**http://www.khoros.unm.edu/staff/neilb/ Weblint.html**) For UNIX fans, Weblint is an HTML version of Lint. This program checks HTML documents for proper syntax and good style. You must download and run this program on your WWW server to evaluate your Web pages.

- HTMLChek (**http://uts.cc.utexas.edu/~churchh/ htmlchek.html**) HTMLChek strictly looks at HTML 2.0 and 3.0 files for HTML and style breaches. The goal of HTMLCheck is to make your home page more rugged and less apt to contain common HTML errors.

V

Final Touches

Chapter 11

World, I'm Here!

Once your home page is finished and available on the Web, hordes and hordes of people will stop by for a look because they want to see it, right? Not if nobody knows about it. Without publicity and home page advertisements, no one will even know that you have a home page, let alone stop by.

That's where this chapter comes into play. In it you'll learn how to announce to the Internet and WWW world that your page is up and raring to have visitors. I'll teach you how to create and place home page advertisements in hot spots around the Internet.

Specifically, in this chapter you learn how to:

- Generate publicity for your home page
- Add your home page to several WWW catalogs
- Use UseNet newsgroups to publicize your home page
- Get other sites to link to your home page

Publicizing Your Web Page

We've all seen the movie *Field of Dreams*. Unfortunately, the "If you build it, they will come" philosophy doesn't work as well on the WWW as it does with baseball ghosts. You've got to do some legwork and spread the word about your home page if you want to attract traffic.

Businesses understand this philosophy, and so should you. When a company creates a brand new product, they generally have to spend thousands (if not millions) of dollars advertising it in magazines, newspapers, and on the television and radio. Fortunately, publicizing your home page is free; your only cost is the time you spend telling other WWW surfers about it. But this time is well spent.

Before you start advertising your home page on the WWW, you should first think through *why* you are publicizing your home page, *who* you are announcing it to, and *what* kind of results to expect. By thinking this through, you'll have a better idea of what your overall goal is behind announcing to the WWW that you have a home page.

> **Note**
>
> Before you can publicize your home page, you've got to upload it onto the Internet. See "Connecting to a Web Provider" in chapter 2 for more information about finding the right spot on the WWW for your home page to situate.

Why Publicize Your Web Page?

For your home page, you're probably advertising for personal satisfaction. Since you installed a counter (see chapter 8), you want to see how many people stop by your home page—it's almost like a contest. Another reason might be because your home page revolves around a particular hobby. You want to publicize your page so other like-minded individuals will stop by. On my home page, for example, I have an entire section on Broadway musicals. When I advertise my Web site, I always mention my musical section so other people who love *Phantom of the Opera* (and others) can see my efforts.

Business home pages usually have ulterior motives. They might advertise their products or services, or simply try to impress visitors. The Coca-Cola home page that I mentioned in chapter 2 is a prime example of this (see fig. 11.1). You're not going to buy soft drinks through the Internet, but just having a WWW presence is good publicity.

Before you go out and scrawl your home page's URL all over the world, make sure you really *want* to advertise your home page. Some Web providers charge based on how many times your home page is accessed (none of the ones listed in appendix A do, but yours might). You might get thousands of people stopping by daily, but it may not be worth the cost. Instead, you might want to tell only a select group of people about your home page.

In fact, many people don't even care about advertising their home page. They use their home page as a personal starting point on the WWW, and customize it for their use only. They create lists of links that interest them, and spots they like to visit. Their home page is more like a home base, where they just check in every now and then. If this is you, why spend lots of time publicizing your home page if you don't care who visits it?

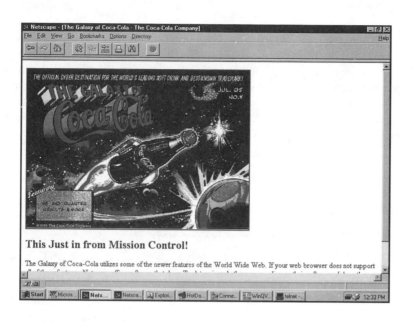

Fig. 11.1
On the WWW, Pepsi drinkers can stay home. Coke is it!

Set Reasonable Expectations

Most likely, advertising your home page will increase the number of visitors you get. Originally, my home page was getting about five visits a day, ranging from my friends to random visitors. Once I started to publicize my home page all over the Internet, my daily tally started increasing rapidly. Eventually, I was averaging around 100 visitors a day. Of course I have no idea whether they liked my home page, found it useful, or ever came back.

Tip

Your Web provider should be able to provide advanced statistics for your home page. They should know how many visits you get, who the visitors are, and whether or not they used any links on your home page.

After awhile, the daily visitor count started to taper off to about 10-15 visits a day. Don't expect basic advertising techniques to attract millions of visitors— set reasonable expectations so you're not disappointed.

Note

While you may be lucky to get a couple of hundred people to visit your home page, some sites get thousands of visitors a day. That's because they offer a unique service

(continues)

V

Final Touches

(continued)

that piques the curiosity of many people, and keeps them coming back again and again. For example, Mirksy's Worst of the Web (**http://turnpike.net/metro/mirsky/Worst.html**) gets thousands of people daily because it is a creative and constantly updated site. See "Keep Your Home Page Alive" in chapter 10 for more information on maintaining interest on your home page.

Using WWW Catalogs and Announcement Services

The easiest and most popular way to advertise your home page is by using existing WWW catalogs, announcement services, and indexes. These places exist to publicize new and popular WWW sites all over the world.

Announcement services are like a town crier standing on the corner. They list loads of new home pages constantly for all of the WWW public to read and see. Every type of home page imaginable is listed in these public pages. Related to announcement services, WWW catalogs create searchable lists of Web pages that they know about. You can search a WWW catalog for a specific topic or key word. Finally, WWW indexes actually go out on their own and search the WWW for new pages. They add every page they find to a huge database and let WWW surfers search for different Web sites.

In this section, I have listed several of the most popular announcement, catalog services, and indexes available, and you'll learn to include your home page in their listings.

Announcement Services

Announcement services such as the Netscape or NCSA What's New pages are publicly available sites that anyone can use to announce their home page. You submit a blurb about your home page, and your information will soon appear on these What's New pages for thousands of WWW surfers to see.

These services receive thousands of submissions weekly. Typically, any type of Web page is accepted and listed in these announcement services. They're a great place to start your home page publicity.

NCSA What's New Page

NCSA What's New Home Page

> **http://www.ncsa.uiuc.edu/SDG/Software/Mosaic/Docs/
> whats-new.html**

Add New Submissions

> **http://www.ncsa.uiuc.edu/SDG/Software/Mosaic/Docs/
> whats-new-form.html**

Mosaic, the world's first popular WWW browser, was created by the folk
s at NCSA (National Center for Supercomputing Applications). Their What's
New Page shown in figure 11.2 below has over 2000 new entries weekly. To
see what's new on the WWW, stop by often, because they update their
What's New list three times weekly (and plan on increasing that number
soon).

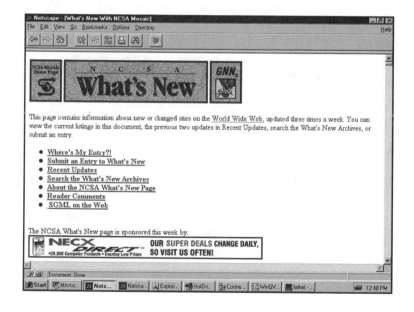

Fig. 11.2
NCSA sponsors
one of the largest
clearinghouses on
the WWW for new
sites.

Submitting your home page to the NCSA What's New listing is and always
has been free. It only takes a few moments. Stop by and fill out the online
form displayed in figure 11.3. All you have to do is type in the name, URL,
category, and a short description of your site. Typically, there is a two-week
delay between submitting your entry and its appearance in the What's New
pages.

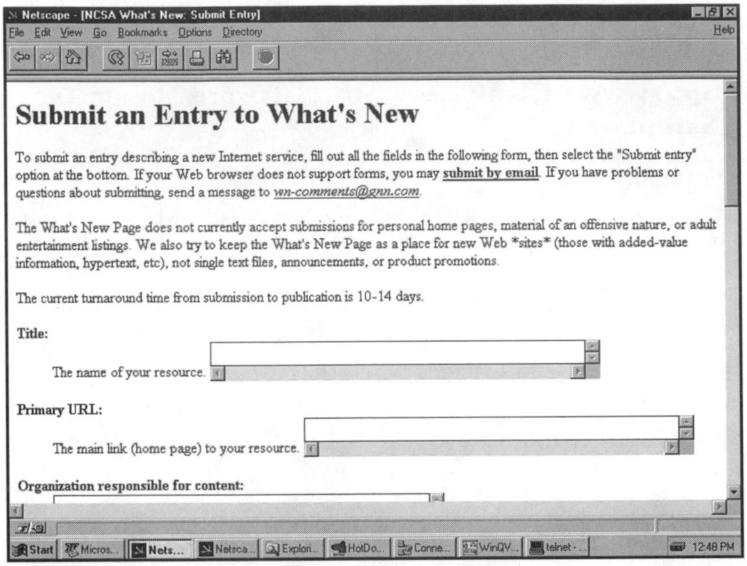

Fig. 11.3
Submitting your
home page is as
easy as 1-2-3.

Tip

If you have trouble submitting your new WWW site via the HTML form (the prefer-
able method), visit **http://www.ncsa.uiuc.edu/SDG/Software/Mosaic/Docs/
whats-new-form-email.html** to learn how to submit via e-mail.

Note

The NCSA What's New page is currently being migrated to the Whole Internet
Catalog's home page located at **http://nearnet.gnn.com/wlc/newrescat
.toc.html**, and may have completely moved by the time you read this book.

What's New at Netscape
Netscape What's New Page
> **http://www.netscape.com/escapes/whats_new.html**

Add New Entries
> **http://www.netscape.com/escapes/submit_new.html**

The Netscape What's New page (see fig. 11.4) is known for listing creative and
innovative Web sites. If you have a really exciting home page, or use HTML
and Netscape in some previously unthought-of fashion, you could be listed

here. Netscape limits the amount of Web sites listed, but getting in the directory can bring you a lot of traffic.

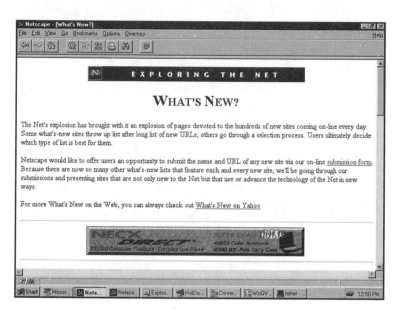

Fig. 11.4
Stop by to see some of the hottest WWW spots available.

Submitting new entries is easy, but don't bother unless your site has something extremely special to offer. Netscape gets thousands of entries, and only a handful make it to their list.

WWW Directories

Unlike announcement services, WWW directories are catalogs of thousands of Web pages. Some, like Yahoo, are organized by category, others are huge listings of home pages. You can stop by these directories and browse or search for a specific entry.

WWW directories are great places to advertise your home page because once your entry is accepted, it will always be listed in the pertinent category. For example, if your home page centers around baseball, you can add it to the Yahoo catalog. Then anyone who searches through the catalog looking for America's favorite pastime will find your home page. You don't have to rely on their reading an announcement page on the right day to see your home page.

Yahoo
Yahoo Directory
    http://www.yahoo.com

Add New Entries
> **http://www.yahoo.com/bin/add**

Yahoo is the biggest, best, and most-used WWW index. Started a couple of years ago by two Stanford University students, Yahoo has grown to become the best spot to find Web sites on nearly every page imaginable. Yahoo is my personal favorite WWW directory, and I use it almost every day. With over 50,000 entries, if a subject isn't listed in the Yahoo directory, you'll likely have trouble finding it elsewhere on the Web.

Anyone can submit entries for their home (or business) pages (see fig. 11.5). You get to choose from the available list of Yahoo categories and then type important information describing your site.

Fig. 11.5
Once you're listed in Yahoo, you'll get a consistent stream of visitors to your home page.

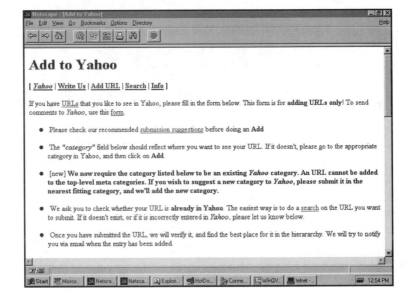

Who's Who on the Internet

Who's Who Personal Pages Directory
> **http://Web.city.ac.uk/citylive/pages.html**

Add Your Home Page
> **http://Web.city.ac.uk/citylive/add.html**

Who's Who on the Internet (WWOTI) is a searchable listing of over 7000 personal home pages from all over the world (see fig. 11.6). Listing only individual home pages, WWOTI strives to be a comprehensive listing of all WWW users with their own Web page. Anyone can add his or her own entry while browsing online.

Unfortunately, WWOTI is limited by an awkward interface. Significant up-
grades are expected, but listing every home page on the Internet is an ardu-
ous task with lots of complications.

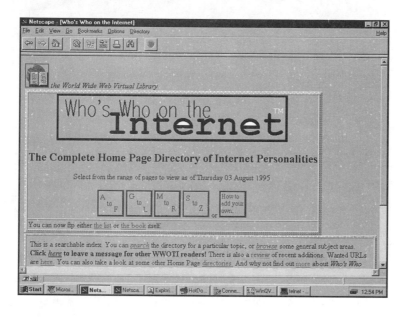

Fig. 11.6
Being listed in
Who's Who isn't
very prestigious
(anyone can join),
but it may draw
some more visits
to your home
page.

Official World Wide Web Yellow Pages

Official Web Yellow Pages
> **http://www.mcp.com/nrp/wwwyp/**

Add New Entries
> **http://www.mcp.com/nrp/wwwyp/submit.html**

Claiming to be the *official* World Wide Web Yellow Pages, this site is spon-
sored by New Riders Press (a sister publisher of Que). You can buy an actual
copy of The Official World Wide Web Yellow Pages and flip through the
organized listings of WWW sites, or search through this online index (whichever is your preference). Remember that the online index is constantly updated and will likely contain up-to-date information.

Shown in figure 11.7, this site resembles your friendly phone book. Users
can search for Web pages by a keyword or category, and even add their own
home page to the list. I recommend including your home page in this directory because of its ever-increasing popularity (and on the next printing, it
will even appear in the book!).

Fig. 11.7
A cyberspace phone book, the WWW Yellow Pages is one of the best directories on the Web.

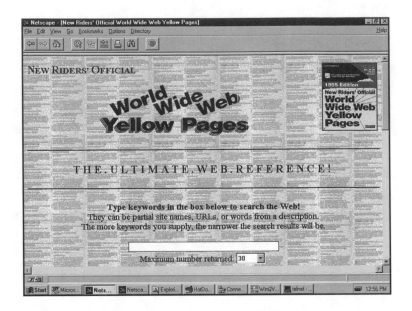

Searching the WWW

Similar to WWW directories, there are several available WWW search tools which will reach out and search thousands of different WWW sites for information. Nicknamed WWW Spiders, these search tools crawl from WWW page to WWW page looking for queried information. They use the links found on one page to bring them to new and different links, thus traveling the WWW like a spider.

I've listed two popular WWW search tools below. You can add your page to these tools and let their WWW spiders creep into your home page!

Lycos

Lycos WWW Page
> **http://lycos.cs.cmu.edu/**

Add New Entries
> **http://lycos.cs.cmu.edu/lycos-register.html**

The Latin word for wolf spider, Lycos boasts that it is *the* catalog of the WWW. Indexing almost 6 million WWW documents, Lycos is constantly traveling the WWW looking for new pages to add to its index (see fig. 11.8). Users can submit a search query and Lycos will return WWW pages according to how well they matched your query.

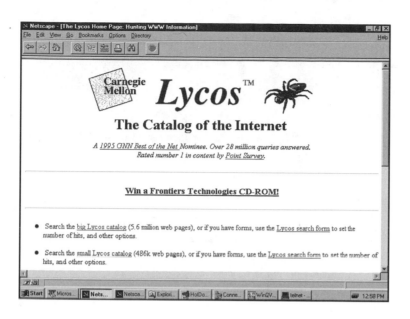

Lycos actively encourages anyone who creates a WWW page to add it to their
index. They want to have the most comprehensive index available. In fact,
Lycos may already have your home page listed. Since their spider is constantly crawling through the Web, it adds new Web pages as they are found,
whether or not you request to be in their index.

Tip

If for some reason you do not want to be included in the Lycos catalog, but the
spider has already found you, choose **delete your own pages** from the Lycos
home page.

Note

The Lycos index is updated weekly. Don't worry if your home page doesn't immediately appear in the searchable index—give it some time to crawl over to your Web
page.

WebCrawler

WebCrawler WWW Index
> **http://Webcrawler.com/**

Add New Entries
> **http://Webcrawler.com/WebCrawler/SubmitURLS.html**

Recently acquired by America Online (AOL), WebCrawler is another popular WWW Search Service (see fig. 11.9). It fields nearly 250,000 searches every month and has visited hundreds of thousands of WWW pages.

You can add your home page to WebCrawler's list of URLs to visit, explore, and index.

Fig. 11.9
Although WebCrawler is smaller than Lycos, it's used extremely often.

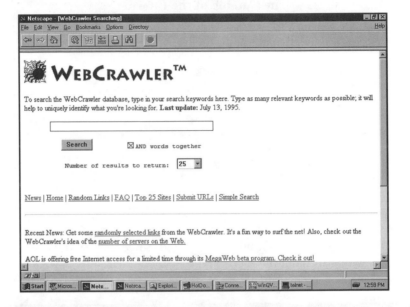

> **Tip**
>
> WebCrawler has a URL pointer that lets visitors go to any page included in its index at random. Similar to a roulette wheel, WebCrawler lets WWW surfers explore new Web sites (maybe even yours) that they have never visited. Click **Random Links** to explore this WWW game of roulette.

Submit It!—17 WWW Catalogs in One

Submit It! Publicity Page
> **http://submit-it.permalink.com/submit-it/**

The fastest and easiest way to publicize your home page on the WWW is using Submit It! This one-stop publicity site lets you fill out one form and submit your home page to 17 of the most popular indexes and catalogs of WWW pages (including Yahoo, Lycos, WebCrawler, and the official WWW Yellow Pages).

Here's how it works. You fill out an entry at the Submit It! site. Automatically, your home page information will be sent to all of the WWW indexes and catalogs shown in figure 11.10. Each site then reads your request and decides whether or not to add your entry.

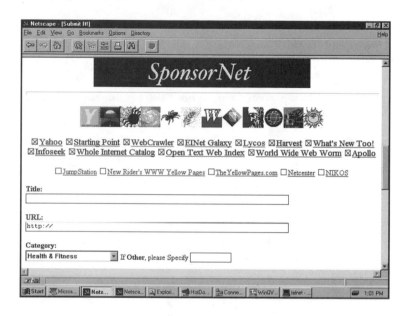

Fig. 11.10
Submit It! lets you add your home page to many WWW catalogs in one shot.

Unfortunately, using Submit It! has several drawbacks. You only get to choose your category once. Each of the catalogs has a slightly different set of categories, so you never get to choose a perfectly optimized category for any of them (which is extremely important for catalogs such as Yahoo).

Additionally, no records are kept letting you know where you have submitted your home page. Also, you might not know whether or not your submission has been accepted. You have to check most of them out individually to see if your home page made it. Still, Submit It! is a great place for you to start publicizing your home page.

Using UseNet Newsgroups

Besides the WWW, newsgroups are one of the most popular applications available on the Internet. Organized into many different categories, newsgroups let people from all over the world hold virtual conversations. I could post a question from my home in Columbus, Ohio, and receive responses from California, Mexico, and Australia.

There are literally thousands of different newsgroups, ranging in interest from Microsoft Windows to automobiles—and covering everything in between. Posting messages to newsgroups is a great way to publicize your home page because it's cheap and reaches a large audience.

comp.infosystems.www.announce

The sole purpose for this newsgroup is to announce new Web pages and HTML services and tools. This is a very high-traffic newsgroup (several hundred posts a week). It is a moderated newsgroup (meaning someone reads every message before it is posted throughout the world), and messages must follow a strict format, or else they'll be rejected.

You can post to comp.infosystems.www.announce directly through Netscape. Go to the following URL:

news:comp.infosystems.www.announce

Then click on the **Post New Article** button at the top of the screen to bring up the Send Mail/Post News dialog box. Type in the message subject and body. Your messages subject should contain one of the words listed below in all caps, followed by an accurate description of what can be found there.

ARCHIVE	ENTERTAINMENT	MAGAZINE	SCIENCE
ART	ENVIRONMENT	MISC	SERVER
BOOK	FAQ	MUSIC	SHOPPING
BROWSER	GAMES	NEWS	SOFTWARE
COLLECTION	HEALTH	PERSONAL	SPORTS
ECONOMY	HUMANITIES	POLITICS	TRANSPORTATION
EDUCATION	INFO	REFERENCE	
EMPLOYMENT	LAW	RELIGION	

If the message's subject is not correct and accurate, the newsgroup posting will be rejected. Here are some examples of good message subjects:

PERSONAL: Andy Shafran's home page about musicals and writing books

SPORTS: The Cincinnati Reds Baseball Team Page

BOOK: Creating Your Own Home Page with Netscape

Likewise, here are some bad message subjects (these would certainly cause messages to be rejected):

PERSONAL: My home page

A simple Web page for my alma mater

Software: Playing games

In your message body, it's important to include the full URL to the page you are announcing. Also, limit the message body to 75 lines (no one will read a message that long anyway). When you're ready, click on the **Send** button. Your posting will appear within 48 hours. Figure 11.11 shows my sample submission.

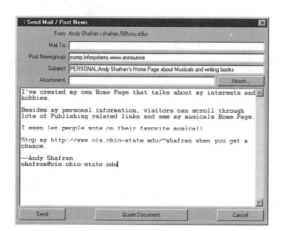

Fig. 11.11
I'm ready to announce my home page.

V

Final Touches

> **Tip**
>
> If you have trouble posting to newsgroups, you can also submit announcements via Internet mail. Include all of the same information in the subject and body and address the message to: **www-announce@boutell.com**.

Personal Newsgroup Interests

Comp.infosystems.www.announce is only the first newsgroup you want to post an announcement message to. Most likely, several other newsgroups will also be interested in knowing about your home page.

Search through your available newsgroups to find others that are related to your home page. Since my page has a lot of information about musicals, I might want to post an announcement to **rec.arts.theatre.musicals** or **alt.stagecraft** to attract like-minded individuals.

Don't forget to check out newsgroups that are local to your city, state, or information provider. The Ohio State University, Columbus, and Ohio all have their own local newsgroups, and since that's where I live, it would be appropriate for me to post a message in them.

Caution

Make sure you don't go overboard in advertising your home page to lots of different newsgroups. Letting people who might be interested in stopping by is acceptable, but posting a message about your home page to every single newsgroup you can find, regardless of its subject, is considered bad etiquette. You'll likely be reprimanded by newsgroup participants.

Other Ways to Advertise Your Home Page

Using WWW catalogs and Internet newsgroups are not the only ways to publicize your home page. These ways may attract a lot of initial attention, but to keep visitors coming to your home page you've got to continually plug it wherever you can (and when it is acceptable).

Resumes and Business Cards

I include my home page's URL on my resume and business cards. Since I'm proud of the work that I've done, I invite clients and prospective business associates to stop by for a visit.

Since home pages are so flexible, I can arrange mine however I feel like. When people stop by, it gives them a chance to learn a lot more about my interests and even lets them send e-mail to me directly.

Here's what my business card looks like:

Signing Your Mail and News Postings

Another popular way of getting the word out is including information in every e-mail message and newsgroup posting you make. At the bottom of every message I send out, I include my name, and the URL of my home page like this:

—Andy Shafran
http://www.cis.ohio-state.edu/~shafran

This lets anyone who reads my message know that I have a home page and where to find it should they want to visit.

Ask Other WWW Sites to Link to You

Another way to attract visitors is by asking people who maintain other pages on similar topics to include a link to your page. For example, there are a lot of other Broadway musical pages out there—mine isn't the only one. Since people who visit one musical page might be inclined to visit others, it only makes sense to try to link all of these related pages together.

Send e-mail to other Web page creators out there who have pages related to yours. Tell them about your home page and give them your URL. Ask them (nicely) to include a link to your page and tell them you will reciprocate. Most likely, they'll be as excited as you are about linking their pages to a new site.

New WWW Developments on the Horizon

The WWW is never standing still. New developments are constantly being announced, and new technologies are continually being created. Since the WWW has a dynamic structure, which is always evolving, you're bound to find a new innovation every time you start exploring.

Recently, several major announcements have been made that will likely change the way the Web works in a few years. Below, I've listed some of the major things you can expect to see down the road. If you think the Web is cool now, wait until you see what's coming!

HTML 3.0

As you are reading this, the current level of HTML is version 2.0 (with the Netscape enhancements). However, it won't be for very long. HTML 3.0 will be released imminently and will greatly increase (and complicate) what you can do with your Web pages. It's anyone's guess when HTML 3.0 will actually be finished, but I'd look for it around the end of 1995 or early 1996. Don't worry, all of your existing pages will look the same under HTML 3.0—the new tags don't interfere with any of the old ones.

Ironically, a lot of new features in HTML 3.0 are already included in Netscape's extensions, which you've learned about in this book. Background images, tables, and text centering capabilities are among that bunch of features. But HTML 3.0 has even more to offer Web page creators. Here's a sample of the new features you can expect to see in HTML 3.0:

- Increased support for Mathematical Equation
- New (and improved) image placement tags
- Official form support (forms aren't included in HTML 2.0)
- Additional layout flexibility
- Style sheets (lots of flexibility for designing how information appears on your pages)

Stop by **http://www.w3.org/hypertext/WWW/Arena/tour/ contents.html** for more information about HTML 3.0 (including when it will be released).

Secure Hypertext Transmissions

Over the past few years, the Internet's popularity has expanded exponentially. Businesses and individuals are clambering to create their own Web pages and join the Information Superhighway.

As more businesses join the WWW, a larger need for private, and secure messages has been created. Currently, sending private information (like credit card numbers) through the WWW is not extremely secure. Just as when you use a cordless phone, anyone who has the right know-how, experience, and drive can listen in and hear your secrets. This poses an enormous threat for banks and businesses who want a very secure way of exchanging financial information, and selling products on the Web.

Recently, new secure communication technologies were pioneered by Netscape (and other companies). These innovations allow you to send encrypted information back and forth across the web. If intercepted, your private data appears jumbled and unreadable, thus allowing you to safely buy things through the Web. Soon you'll be able to do much of your purchasing, banking, and bill paying through the Internet and the WWW.

Stop by **http://home.netscape.com/newsref/std/credit.html** to read more about this secure way of transferring private information.

Java

Not your ordinary cup of coffee, Java is a programming language developed by Sun Microsystems to add stupendous interactive effects to the WWW. Using Java, you can add animation, special effects, and even interactive images to your Web pages.

Still in alpha development (it has a while to go before its release is finalized), Java introduces a new way of thinking about the WWW. Instead of downloading separate animation and audio clips as in HTML 2.0 (you've got to load separate programs to see and listen to them), WWW browsers that support Java can include all of these special effects on the same page without interfering with those Web browsers that don't support Java.

Here's how it works. If I use Netscape to visit a home page with Java-effects built in, I might see a regular WWW page that talks about a chemistry experiment. The headlines appear at the top and tables and images are lined up properly. But if I visit that same page with a Java-supported browser (currently, HotJava—Sun's WWW browser is the only one that supports Java), I might not recognize the page. Part of it could display a video clip of the chemistry experiment in action and words might sweep on and off the page. Sounds pretty neat, huh? It is.

Java promises to be one of the greatest innovations the WWW has seen. Even better, Netscape announced that subsequent versions of their WWW browser would include built-in Java support. Soon the whole Web will have a mocha smell about it! Unfortunately, creating Java-specific pages and applications is complicated—it is similar to writing a C++ program.

Stop by the Java home page (**http://java.sun.com**) to learn more about the development project. You won't be disappointed.

VRML

Short for Virtual Reality Modeling Language, VRML provides a visual and interactive interface to the WWW. VRML activists believe that the Web should be seen, not read. VRML wants you to be able to walk into a Web site and point at the information you want to see.

Instead of linking text to other HTML home pages, VRML offers a fluid graphical interface towards experiencing things. One perfect use of VRML would be to shop at a grocery store. From your home, you could log onto your local store. With your mouse, you can walk down each aisle and pick up various items to put in your shopping cart. If you wanted to see the nutritional information of yogurt, you'd pick up the package, turn it over and take a look. VRML offers all the benefits of being there, *without actually being there*.

Start learning about VRML at **http://vrml.wired.com**. This was the original VRML site and has important links to VRML sites all over the world. For a sneak peek at VRML, figure 11.12 shows the first Windows-based VRML browser (**http://www.webmaster.com:80/vrml/wvwin/**) in action.

Fig. 11.12
Virtual Reality is
here today and
ready to be used!

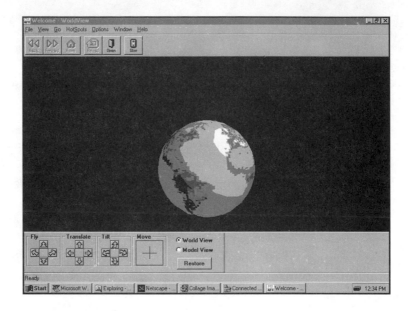

Appendix A

Affordable Web Providers

This is a brief appendix of recommended Web providers that will let you put your home page on their site. Read through the list because each Web provider is slightly unique and different. Their prices range from free to $11.37 a month and each one has its own home page file limitations. Any of these sites listed are affordable, and you can't go too wrong. Whether or not you use one of these, or your own Internet/Web provider, make sure you comparison shop prices and the services you are looking for.

Read my comments on each listing for a brief summary of the pros and cons of each Web Provider. Good luck, and I'll see you surfing on the web!

Geocities—Beverly Hills Pages

For a basic home page, this is the best site listed. Everything here is free, from creating your home page to monthly (even daily) maintenance. Sharp limitations on your home page file size, not much technical support, and few advanced home page features limit this site to beginning users only.

The best part of this site is the price. The people who run this site believe that every Internet user deserves his or her own *free* home page as a personal starting spot on the Internet.

Company URL:	http://www.geopages.com/BHI/
Monthly Charge:	Free
Disk Space:	200k (.2 Meg)
Maintenance Charges:	None
E-mail Address:	sales@bhi90210.com

Built in home page editor lets you create decent looking home pages in just a few minutes. You'll want to use Hotdog to create snazzy pages on your own.

■ FTP access to update your home page instantly

ProTech Specialists, Inc.

Worldwide Web Consulting

This friendly Web provider will go out of its way to help you get your home page up and running immediately. Affordable costs and free monthly maintenance make this site a good option. File size and page size limited for lowest monthly rate. Affordable and professional Web consulting services are also available.

Company URL:	http://www.pspec.com
Monthly Charges:	$5.00 page/month (a page is whatever will fit on one side of an 8 1/2 x 11 page)
Disk Space:	See above
Maintenance Charges:	Free, once per month
E-mail Address:	protech@pspec.com

Additional Information:

- No setup fee for home pages (when you supply the text and image files).

- Setup support available.

- First two months free for readers of this book.

Web Works

This site is an excellent option for the Internet user who knows how to create a web page and doesn't need much hand-holding. For $5 a month you get a 2 meg home page file size limit and unlimited FTP access to maintain your home page.

It's my first choice of all the pay services listed here.

Company URL:	http://wworks.com
Monthly Charge/per Meg:	$5/month (payable quarterly)
Disk Space:	2 meg limit
Maintenance Charges:	Unlimited FTP access
E-mail Address:	sales@wworks.com

Additional Information:

- An FTP account to maintain your pages

- Access to a directory of tools (editors, image tools, etc.)

- Your home page URL will look like: http://wworks.com/<user name>

Ripco

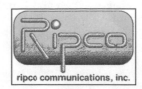

This company may charge slightly more than some others in this list, but you get much more for the price. Their $35 quarterly fee includes full SLIP access to browse the Internet and create and maintain your own home page.

The file limit is an astounding 7 megs, which earns this spot a second look if you are creating a larger, more robust home page.

Company URL:	http://www.ripco.com/ripco/
Monthly Charge/per Meg:	$11.67/month (prepaid, 3 months at $35 total)
Disk Space:	7 megs ($1/Meg/month for additional space)
Maintenance Charges:	Included with your SLIP access
E-mail Address:	info@ripco.com

Additional Information:

- Telnet/dialup shell, full UseNet, e-mail, FTP, SLIP/PPP
- T1 Internet connection (fast)
- Ideal combined Internet & Web provider.

NJ Computer Connection (NJCC)

Here's an excellent site that caters to new Internet and WWW users. It offers reasonable pricing and file space, and promises to gently lead new users into the Internet. It is a full service Internet & Web Provider.

Company URL: http://www.njcc.com/

Monthly Charge/per Meg: $7.95 a month - $79.96/year
                             ($9.95 startup fee)

Disk Space: 5 megs ($4.95 for an additional 5 megs)

Maintenance Charges: Unlimited access for free

E-mail Address: account@pluto.njcc.com

Additional Information:

- Several levels of accounts available to provide Internet access to all sorts of users.

- Customized and updated hotlists provide perfect starting point for any WWW user.

Loginet Incorporated

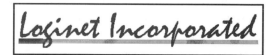

One look at this home page, and you know that this site understands good Web page design. Nice integration of graphics and text makes it easy to use and sets your mind at ease for using it for your WWW needs. It offers high file limits and several pricing plans. Stop by and see if it fits your budget.

Company URL: http://www.loginet.com

Monthly Charge/per Meg: $10/month ($20 startup fee)

Disk Space: 10 meg limit

E-mail Address: new-accounts@loginet.com

Additional Information:

- Attractive home page shows that this site understands web design

- Several pricing plans ranging from personal to business usage.

Prodigy

With Prodigy's interface, you also get a free web page with unlimited file space as part of your monthly membership fee of $9.95. Be careful, though—at $2.95 an hour, Prodigy can add up really quickly.

You get all the news, weather, sports, and family info that prodigy has, and a web page, for the same price of several of the other providers listed here.

Company URL: http://antares.prodigy.com

Monthly Charge/per Meg: $9.95 for 5 hours + $2.95 for additional hours

Disk Space: According to Prodigy, virtually unlimited

Maintenance Charges: Your hourly charges

Additional Information:

Prodigy has several built in templates that make creating a simple (but crude) home page a matter of minutes. Jump to **home page** once you're online or go to **http://pages.prodigy.com**.

Call 1-800-776-3449 for a free Prodigy sign up kit that includes a free month and 10 hours online (it took me three to get set up and installed).

COMPUNET SERVICES, INC.

I included this site because they are professional Web developers. As an end user, you can get a special offer on monthly home page rates, or pay their consulting fees for a professionally designed page.

After seeing how many design rules their home page breaks (they use "click here" as a HyperText link, and don't use transparent GIFS with their color backgrounds), you're better off creating your own home page and paying them just to put it up on the web.

Company URL:	http://www.csnet.com
Monthly Charge:	$10/ Month for 1MB.
Disk Space:	$8/Per additional meg
Maintenance Charges:	First month is free. After that, a nominal fee or $50.00 an hour
E-mail Address:	info@csnet.com

Additional Information:

- Home page design and development services

- Can install and run a special Web Server just for you and your needs.

- Support CGI scripting for advanced HTML commands such as Forms and Image Maps.

Appendix B

References Used In This Book

This appendix consists of the links that I've talked about and used throughout this book, including examples and references. I've organized them by category so you can easy scan through this list for links useful to you.

Useful Home Page Links

HTML 2.0 Definition
http://www.w3.org/hypertext/WWW/MarkUp/html-spec/html-pubtext.html

The Hotdog Home Page
http://www.sausage.com

WWW Browsers

Netscape—Browser used in this book
http://home.netscape.com

Mosaic—Another popular graphical browser
http://www.ncsa.uiuc.edu/SDG/Software/SDGSoftDir.html

Lynx—Text only browser
http://www.cc.ukans.edu/about_lynx/about_lynx.html

Arena—HTML 3.0 browser
http://www.w3.org/hypertext/WWW/Arena/

HTML Validation Tools

The HAL Validation Service
http://www.halsoft.com/html-val-svc/

Weblint: the HTML style and syntax checker
http://www.khoros.unm.edu/staff/neilb/weblint.html

HTMLChek—Another validation tool
http://uts.cc.utexas.edu/~church/htmlchek.html

MOMSpider—automatic checks links
http://www.ics.uci.edu/WebSoft/MOMspider/

Checker—also checks links automatically
http://www.ugrad.cs.ubc.ca/spider/q7f192/branch/checker.html

Home Page Counters

Easy Counter used in this book
http://www.forsmark.uu.se/counter.html

A step by step tutorial on adding counters to your Web page
http://purgatory.ecn.purdue.edu:20002/JBC/david/how.html

Add a counter to your Web server
http://melmac.corp.harris.com/access_counts.html

Cool WWW pages

"The Net" Home Page
http://www.spe.sony.com/Pictures/SonyMovies/netmulti.html

Microsoft's Technical Support Page
http://www.microsoft.com/Support/

The Internet Mall
http://www.imall.com/homepage.html

The Crime Scene Evidence File
http://odin.cbu.edu/~vaskin/crime/crime.html

ESPN Sportszone
http://espnet.sportszone.com/

Coca Cola Company
http://www.cocacola.com/

The Weather Channel's Home Page
http://www.infi.net/weather

Mirksy's Worst of the Web
http://turnpike.net/metro/mirsky/Worst.html

An interactive tour through the Louvre
http://www.emf.net/wm/paint/auth/michelangelo/

Que's Home Page
http://www.mcp.com/que/

***Politically Correct Bedtime Stories*, by James Finn Garner**
http://www.mcp.com/general/news6/polit.html

The Brang Home Page (bad multimedia page)
http://www.inch.com/~mick/home/brang.html

Star Trek Voyager Home Page
http://voyager.paramount.com/VoyagerActive.html

Andy Shafran's (mine) Home Page
http://www.cis.ohio-state.edu/~shafran/

Roxanne's Home Page
http://www.geopages.com/CapitolHill/1099/

Multimedia Clips and Information

Audio Clip Sites
http://sunsite.unc.edu/pub/multimedia/sun-sounds/movies/
http://ai.eecs.umich.edu/people/kennyp/sounds.html
http://web.msu.edu/vincent/index.html
http://www.acm.uiuc.edu/rml/

Audio File Format FAQ
http://www.cis.ohio-state.edu/hypertext/faq/usenet/audio-fmts/top.html

Video Clip Sites
http://w3.eeb.ele.tue.nl/mpeg/index.html
http://www.acm.uiuc.edu/rml/
http://deathstar.rutgers.edu/people/bochkay/movies.html

MPEG Specifications
http://www.cis.ohio-state.edu/hypertext/faq/usenet/mpeg-faq/top.html

QT Technical Specifications
http://www.cast.uni-linz.ac.at/st/staff/rm/QTquickcam/

AVI Technical Information
http://www.microsoft.com

Publicity Links

NCSA What's New Home Page
http://www.ncsa.uiuc.edu/SDG/Software/Mosaic/Docs/whats-new.html

Netscape What's New Page
http://www.netscape.com/escapes/whats_new.html

Yahoo Directory
http://www.yahoo.com

Who's Who on the Internet Directory
http://web.city.ac.uk/citylive/pages.html

Official Web Yellow Pages
http://www.mcp.com/nrp/wwwyp/

Lycos WWW Page
http://lycos.cs.cmu.edu/

WebCrawler WWW Index
http://webcrawler.com/

Submit It! Publicity Page
http://submit-it.permalink.com/submit-it/

WWW Announcements newsgroup
news:comp.infosystems.www.announce

New Web Technologies

HTML 3.0 Definition
http://www.w3.org/hypertext/WWW/MarkUp/html3-dtd.txt

Java
http://java.sun.com/

VRML
http://vrml.wired.com/

Appendix C

Home Page Final Check List

Listed below is a final checklist you should use when you're just about finished creating your home page. Before you make it publicly available, run through this simple checklist to make sure you've caught most of the common mistakes new home page creators make. Below, I've summarized some of the common tips and tricks that I talked about throughout the book.

Basic HTML

The important <HTML> </HTML>, <HEAD> </HEAD>, and <BODY> </BODY> tags are included on my home page

My home page is properly titled using the <TITLE> and </TITLE> tags

All of my HTML tags have their respective closing tags (i.e. <H1> and </H1>)

My home page shows my name and e-mail address and the date that the page was last changed.

The <P> is used to separate my paragraphs of text (instead of nothing or the <BR> tag)

The <BLINK> tag is used sparingly

Lists and Tables

I've replaced large paragraphs with lists and tables wherever I could

I used the TAB key to line up my lists and each list item in my HTML source file so I know which items are in which list

All the rows in my table have the same amount of columns and vice versa

I use row and column headers in my tables

Links

I don't overuse WWW links on my home page by linking virtually every word

I make important words and phrases hot so visitors know where they're linking

All of my links have been recently tested and work properly

Links to large images and audio and video files are labeled with the size of the file they download

My internal targets use descriptive names inside of my home page and the links to them work correctly

Images

All of my home page images are around 20K or fewer

My entire home page, images and all, is smaller than 100K

Images larger than 20K have smaller, thumbnail size images on my home page that link visitors to the larger images

The full path and file name to all of my images is correct

My background pattern isn't too busy and confusing

I can read text placed on top of my background pattern without straining my eyes

My images properly align with the text next to them

Other

I've looked at my home page in Netscape before making it available online

There are no misspelled words on my home page

I used HTML comments to make notes to myself for future updates

My HTML source file is readable and easy to update

I have placed a backup of my home page and all associated files (images, audio, etc.) in a safe place—just in case

Appendix D

What's on the CD-ROM?

You need three things when you build your own Web page; Web page building materials, tools, and creativity. The *Creating Your Own Netscape Web Pages* CD-ROM provides you with an extensive collection of materials and tools for building your own Web page. However, you must supply the creativity. We've also included a lot of other useful goodies such as viewers and compression programs in the CD-ROM. All of the materials and programs are easy to browse through and download right through your Web browser.

Browse the CD

Browse the *Creating Your Own Netscape Web Pages* CD-ROM through Web pages. You can easily access everything on the CD by firing up your Web browser and loading APPCD.HTM from the CD. For instance, if your CD-ROM drive is drive D, then the URL is file:D:\appcd.htm. Or, under Netscape, click on the **File menu** and select **Open File** to open the Open dialog box. Select your CD-ROM drive in the **Look In drop down list**, click on **APPCD**, and click the **Open** button.

You'll find mostly four types of links on each Web page: links to other pages, links to materials or applications, links to folders on the CD, and links to resources on the Internet (as shown in fig. D.1).

On the Buttons page you can see the link to the BUTTONS folder filled with buttons files on the CD-ROM. The mouse cursor (pointing hand) is pointing to the BUTTONS folder. Below the BUTTONS folder are two links to Web pages on the Internet: Christian Morgensen's Home Page and Chris World.

Fig. D.1
Files in the
BUTTONS folder
on the CD-ROM.

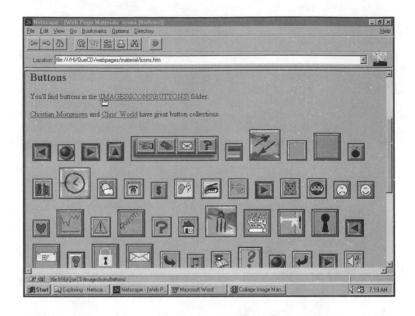

When you click on a link to a folder, either the folders contents are loaded into the browser, as shown in figure D.2, or a separate folder window is opened up (depending on the browser that you use). In either case, you can easily view any file in the folder by double clicking it, or you can copy the file to your hard drive using the method usual for your particular browser. (In Netscape, hold down your **Shift** button and click on the file. A Save As dialog box will open. Then follow the usual procedures. If you're using the Microsoft Internet Browser, drag-and-drop the files.)

Fig. D.2
Here are four types
of links accessible
from Web pages.

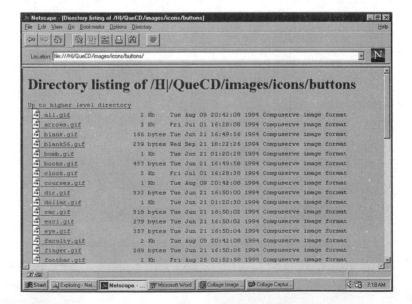

Installing and Saving Files onto Your Computer

Install programs onto your computer by clicking the link associated with To install [this program] click here, under Installation Instructions.

If you're using Netscape the Unknown File Type dialog box will appear. Netscape doesn't offer a good way to launch individual programs through links. However, you can fool it into doing a pretty good job. Here's how.

1. Choose Preferences from the Options menu to open the Preferences dialog box and click the Helper Apps tab.

2. Scroll down and highlight application/octet-stream in the file type list.

3. Click the Launch the Application radio button. It's one of the Action radio buttons toward the bottom of the Preferences dialog box.

4. Click the OK button.

Now when you click on a link to a setup program the Save As dialog box appears. Click the Cancel button and you should see a setup program launch. Follow the setup programs instructions.

If you're using the Microsoft Internet Explorer you don't need to do any of the above. When you click on a setup program link, the Confirm File Open dialog box appears. To launch the setup program simply click the Open File button.

Sometimes you need to copy program files to your computer. When you click on a linked file that you want to copy under Netscape the Unknown File Type dialog box usually pops up. Click the Save To Disk button and go through the usual Save As dialog box procedures. Sometimes Netscape tries to load a file that you want to save. You can get Netscape to give you the Save As dialog box by holding down the Shift key while you click on the link to the program that you want to save.

Under the Microsoft Internet Explorer the Confirm File Open dialog box will appear when you click on a link to a file that you want to save to disk. Click the Save As button and go through the usual Save As dialog box procedures to save the file to your hard disk.

Web Page Materials

Like any building project, you must begin with good raw materials to build a good Web page. This section is a good place to start with a wide array of icons, background images, templates, and links to sites on the Web.

Much of the building materials on the CD are linked to pages that you can browse with your Web browser. All that you need to do is point and click on what you want to get at. However, there's simply too much material to link it all to Web pages so you'll find linked folders on each page. When you click on them, they will open, showing all of the relevant material. Double-click on any file that you want to examine and it'll load into your browser.

Audio

Choose from hundreds of audio files. You'll find the following general categories of sounds on the CD:

- Animal sounds

- Special effects

- Sounds from around the house

- Instrument sounds

- Sounds from nature

- Voices

Links to sound archives on the Internet are included.

If you're using Netscape don't forget to set up a helper application to run WAV format sound files!

Hotlists

Use the Hotlists page to access major Web page building resources on the Internet. Most of these links will take you to huge repositories of link lists to Internet resources useful to a Web page builder. Check out the Macmillan Winner's Circle page through the link at the bottom of the Hotlists page under Best Personal Web Page Contest. You can look at the winning Web page and enter your Web page into the contest.

Images

There are hundreds of images for you on this CD, including the following:

- Backgrounds
- Bullets
- Buttons
- Lines
- Pictures

Usually there are far too many images to include them all on the page, so be sure to check out the folders. Also, explore the links to Internet sites and lists on the Internet that'll take you to even more sites.

Template

Andy Shafran, the author of this book, has included a template for you to start you off with a working Web page (including a link to Andy's home page). You can also open any of the nearly seventy Web pages included on this CD to check out how something is done or borrow pieces of code. You can do this in Netscape by choosing View in the menu and clicking on S once. Youll find most of the Web pages under the \WEBPAGES\ folder on the CD. Just open the files with the HTM extension using any word processor.

Video

We included both QuickTime and MPEG videos for you to try out. When you open the Video page just click on a linked picture. The movie will load onto your computer and run if your browser is configured to run a program that will view the video type you clicked on. Otherwise, you can either save the video file onto your hard disk or you can configure a viewer. You'll find both QuickTime and MPEG viewers on this CD. Just look under Internet-Related Applications, Viewers.

Tools for Building Web Pages

The right tools are essential to the builder of Web pages. We've included a large assortment of HTML Editors, Image Map Editors, and HTML converters on the CD, along with links to some useful sites on the Web.

HTML Converters

These files convert pre-existing files into the HTML format.

RTF to HTML

Use this utility to convert documents from the RTF format to HTML. RTF (Rich Text Format) is becoming the standard format used for text under Windows, especially Windows 95, where the standard word processor included with the operating system, WordPad, handles RTF. Most major word processors can import and export RTF files. This package includes a Microsoft Word 2.0 for Windows template for writing HTML.

Its location on the CD is:

    \APPS\CONVERT\RTF2HTML\

Tex2RTF

Use this utility to convert LaTeX files to HTML. Tex2RTF also converts LaTeX to Windows Help file format if you need that capability. LaTeX is a format that's very popular for files created for print and online, and is also a common language used for technical documents. To make the most of Tex2RTF you should read through the program's very good help system.

Its location on the CD is:

    \APPS\CONVERT\TEX2RTF\

HTML Editors

Using HTML Editors will speed up your HTML coding.

HotDog Web Editor

For a fast, flexible, and friendly way to create HTML documents, use the HotDog Web Editor. HotDog supports both Netscape extensions to HTML and proposed HTML 3.0 elements. Its dialogs let you perform complex tasks like creating forms and tables in a few seconds. And HotDog includes many features like finding duplicate tags and converting DOS files for use on UNIX systems. You can easily set almost 50 options to set up HotDog to behave just the way you want it to.

Its location on the CD is:

    \APPS\HTML\HOTDOG\

HTML Assistant for Windows

HTML Assistant is a simple shareware HTML document editor. Most commands are implemented via a huge toolbar. The program is a good editor for small documents limited to 32K files. A unique feature of HTML Assistant is its ability to convert files that contain URLs to HTML documents that can be read with any Web browser.

Its location on the CD is:

    \APPS\HTML\HTMLASST\

HTMLed

HTMLed is a powerful shareware HTML document editor that features a toolbar and abundant and clear menus.

Its location on the CD is:

    \APPS\HTML\HTMLED\

HTML Easy! Pro

You can easily make a Web page with HTML Easy! Pro. You can also use HTML Easy! Pro as a text editor. HTML Easy! Pro supports full HTML 3.0 commands and Netscape Extensions.

Its location on the CD is:

    \APPS\HTML\HTMLEASY\

HTML HyperEdit

HTML HyperEdit is a simple editor that includes a hypermedia tutorial.

Its location on CD is:

    \APPS\HTML\HTMLHYP\

HTML Writer

HTML Writer is a stand-alone HTML authoring program. Most HTML tags can be inserted using an extensive set of menu commands. A toolbar is used to implement many HTML tags. Another feature is HTML Editor's support of templates, which you can use to help design and create HTML documents with a consistent look and feel.

Its location on the CD is:

    \APPS\HTML\HTMLWRIT\

Live Markup

Build or edit Web pages in the actual HTML environment directly on-screen without the necessity to learn or type any HTML tags with Live Markup. Live Markup is a WISIWYG (What You See Is What You Get) HTML editor.

Its location on the CD is:

\APPS\HTML\LIVEMARK\

SoftQuad HoTMetaL

SoftQuad HoTMetal is a full-featured, professional-quality HTML editor. With this freeware, you can edit multiple documents at the same time, use templates to ensure consistency between documents, and use its powerful word-processor-like features.

Its location on the CD is:

\APPS\HTML\HOTMETAL\

WebEdit v1.1a

WebEdit allows you to edit multiple documents at once. It has a very clean, simple interface that hides powerful features.

Its location on the CD is:

\APPS\HTML\WEBEDIT\

WebForms v1.5

Create your own forms and link them to your home page with WebForms. Responses to the forms you create are automatically sent to your mailbox, then read by WebForms and collected in a Response Database.

Its location on the CD is:

\APPS\HTML\WEBFORMS\

HTML Editors for MS Word

If you're a Microsoft Word user you can turn the familiar word processor into an HTML editor.

ANT_HTML

Create hypertext documents using the ANT_DEMO template for Microsoft Word 6 for Windows and Macintosh. You can insert HTML codes into any new or existing Word or ASCII document. ANT_DEMO is a demonstration version of the ANT_PLUS conversion utility and the ANT_HTML package. Both ANT_HTML and ANT_PLUS work in all international versions of Word 6.

Its location on the CD is:

>   \APPS\HTML\ANT_DEMO\

CU_HTML

Create HTML documents in Microsoft Word 2 or 6 using the CU_HTML template.

Its location on the CD is:

>   \APPS\HTML\CU_HTML\

GT_HTML

GT_HTML is a Microsoft Word 6 template for creating HTML documents. Only a small number of HTML tags are currently supported by GT_HTML, but the ones that are included are the most common tags and should be useful for many basic HTML documents.

Its location on the CD is:

>   \APPS\HTML\GT_HTML\

HTML Author

HTML Author is a template for creating HTML documents in Microsoft Word 6.

Location on CD

>   \APPS\HTML\HTMLAUTH\

Microsoft Internet Assistant for Word 6

Create HTML documents visually using Microsoft Internet Assistant for Word 6 for Windows. HTML tags are hidden and created automatically by the Internet Assistant. Internet Assistant also turns Word into a Web browser.

Its location on the CD is:

>   \APPS\HTML\WORDIA\

Microsoft Internet Assistant for Word for Windows 95

Create HTML documents visually, using Microsoft Internet Assistant for Word for Windows 95. HTML tags are hidden and created automatically by the Internet Assistant. Internet Assistant also turns Word into a Web browser.

Its location on the CD is:

>   \APPS\HTML\WORDIA7\

WebWizard

WebWizard is an HTML authoring system that works as a template in Microsoft Word 6. A new toolbar is added to Word 6 with some HTML commands and a new WebWizard menu is added to the menu bar.

Its location on the CD is:

   \APPS\HTML\WEBWIZAR\

Image Map Editors

Simplify making image maps by using an image map editor.

Mapedit

Map images using the WYSIWYG (What You See Is What You Get) image mapper Mapedit.

Its location on CD is:

   \APPS\HTML\MAPEDIT\

Map THIS!

Map images with Map THIS!

Its location on the CD is:

   \APPS\HTML\MAPTHIS\

Internet-Related Applications

Materials and tools will give you most of what you need to build Web pages. Nevertheless, these additional applications come in handy when you spend a lot of time on the Web. You may want to turn your PC into a Web server or you might need a viewer for a file type that you hadn't viewed before.

Internet Access Provider/Netscape Browser

If you need an Internet access provider, try out Earthlink. Everything is here to get you up and running, including a Netscape browser.

Its location on the CD is:

   \APPS\EARTHLNK\

Viewers: Pictures, Sound, Video, and PostScript

View any file on the Internet by having the right viewers.

GhostView v1.0

Use GhostView version 1.0 to view printer files that conform to GhostScript 2.6 or later standards. GhostScript is an interpreter for the PostScript page-description language used by many laser printers. GhostView can also be used to print GhostScript-embedded documents.

Its location on the CD is:

    \APPS\VIEWERS\GSVIEW\

Jasc Media Center

Use Jasc Media Center to keep large collections of multimedia files organized. The program supports 37 file formats, including GIF, JPEG, MIDI, WAV, and AVI. Formats that aren't supported can still be used if you have an external file filter for them.

Its location on the CD is:

    \APPS\VIEWERS\JASCMEDI\

LView

Load, view, edit, and save image files of many different formats with LView.

Its location on the CD is:

    \APPS\VIEWERS\LVIEW\

Media Blastoff

View several popular graphics formats, as well as sound and movies, with Media Blastoff.

Its location on the CD is:

    \APPS\VIEWERS\BLASTOFF\

MPegPlay

Play MPEG movies with MPegPlay. MPegPlay is a 32-bit program and will run under Windows 95 and Windows NT. You must use Win32s to run it under 16-bit Windows.

Its location on the CD is:

    \APPS\VIEWERS\MPEGPLAY\

PlayWave

Use PlayWave to play WAV sound files. PlayWave can be set to loop a wave file continuously.

Its location on the CD is:

\APPS\VIEWERS\PLAYWAVE\

QuickTime 2.0 for Windows

Play QuickTime movies (MOV) with QuickTime 2.0 for Windows. MOV files are common on the Internet.

Its location on the CD is:

\APPS\VIEWERS\QTIME20\

VuePrint

Work with and view graphics in several popular formats including JPEG and GIF using VuePrint. The screen saver included with VuePrint displays image file collections. VuePrint also has a built-in UUEncoder and UUDecoder. VuePrint is an all-in-one graphics solution for most of your Internet graphics needs.

Its locations on the CD are:

\APPS\VIEWERS\VUEPRINT\WIN31\

\APPS\VIEWERS\VUEPRINT\WINNT\

WinECJ

WinECJ is a fast JPEG viewer. The program can open multiple files and has a slide-show-presentation mode.

Its location on the CD is:

\APPS\VIEWERS\WINECJ\

WPlany

WPlany plays several sound file formats found on the Internet including WAV. WPlany is an easy-to-use program.

Its location on the CD is:

\APPS\VIEWERS\WPLANY\

Web Servers

Turn your PC into a Web server.

Web4Ham

Web4Ham turns your PC into a Web site that other people can access with any Web-browsing software.

Its location on the CD is:

\APPS\WWW\WEB4HAM\

Windows HTTPD v1.4

Windows HTTPD has extensive online documentation in HTML format. Run only under Microsoft Windows and Windows for Workgroups 3.1 and 3.11.

Its location on the CD is:

\APPS\WWW\WHTTPD\

Web Accessories

Here are a couple of programs to make your Web life easier.

Launcher

Launcher allows you to launch a Microsoft Windows application from a link in a Web browser. This feature allows you to open a Windows application without creating a link to a particular document.

Its location on the CD is:

\APPS\WWW\LAUNCHER\

URL Grabber Demo

If you've ever read an article in a UseNet newsgroup or an e-mail message and seen a URL that you wanted to save for further reference, then you can use URL Grabber. Sure, you can copy and paste the URL into a browser and then save it in a hotlist or bookmark, but this handy little utility makes this process even easier.

The URL Grabber toolbar enables you to grab a URL from documents as you read them and then save a collection of addresses as HTML documents that you can open in any Web browser. You then have a Web document that contains all the links to the URL addresses that you've saved, enabling you to jump to those URLs quickly and easily. (In this demo version, you are limited to grabbing three addresses each time you run the program.)

Its location on the CD is:

\APPS\WWW\GRABDEMO\

Other Applications

Don't let this other category on the CD fool you. These are probably the most used applications both on and off the Web.

Compression Software

Everyone uses compression software whether they know it or not. (Almost all software that you buy, such as Microsoft Windows, is stored as compressed files and is decompressed when installed.) File compression saves a lot of time and money by decreasing file transfer times over the Net.

ArcMaster

Use ArcMaster to compress and decompress files in many popular compression formats, including ZIP, LHZ, and ARJ. You need to have the file compression/decompression utilities for each of these. ArcMaster is a front end program that makes it easier to use the DOS utilities under Windows. It supports drag-and-drop, allows you to conveniently manipulate compressed files, and converts files from one compression format to another.

Its location on the CD is:

\APPS\COMPRESS\ARCMASTR\

ArcShell

ArcShell is a Windows shell you can use to make it easy to manipulate ZIP, LHZ, ARC, and ARJ compression files. You need to have the file compression/ decompression utilities for each of these. ArcShell acts as a front end to the DOS utilities.

Its location on the CD is:

\APPS\COMPRESS\ARCSHELL\

Drag And Zip

Turn your Windows 3.1 File Manager into a file manager for creating and managing ZIP, LZH, and GZ files by using the Drag And Zip utilities. Drag And Zip has built-in routines to zip and unzip files that makes it very easy to compress and extract ZIP files. Drag And Zip supports copies of PKZIP, LHA, and GUNZIP to manage compressed files and has a built-in virus scanner that you can use to scan compressed files for possible viruses.

Its location on the CD is:

\APPS\COMPRESS\DRAGZIP\

WinZip

Use WinZip 6.0 to painlessly zip and unzip files. This version has been specially developed for Windows 95. For instance, use the Add To Zip command added to Explorers context menu to quickly add files to an archive. Drag-and-drop is also supported.

Its location on the CD is:

\APPS\COMPRESS\WINZIP\

Zip Manager

Zip Manager is a stand-alone Windows ZIP utility. Zip Manager doesn't require PKZIP and PKUNZIP and is 100 percent PKZIP 2.04 compatible.

Its locations on the CD are:

\APPS\COMPRESS\ZIPMGR\WIN31\

\APPS\COMPRESS\ZIPMGR\WINNT\

Zip Master

Use Zip Master to add, freshen, or update existing ZIP files, create new ZIP files, extract from or test existing ZIP files, view existing ZIP file contents, and many other functions. Zip Master doesn't require you to have PKZIP or PKUNZIP.

Its location on the CD is:

\APPS\COMPRESS\ZIPMASTR\

Picture Conversion/Manipulation

Graphics is one of the things that makes the Web so intuitive and fun. So its not surprising that a Web builder will often use picture conversion and manipulation programs. In addition to the programs here, many of the Viewers under Internet-Related Applications are also able to convert and manipulate images.

Image'n'Bits

Use Image'n'Bits to manipulate and convert graphics. Among the formats supported are BMP and GIF. Image'n'Bits is able to create special effects including dithering, pixelizing, and solarizing. If you're working with artistic images or photographs Image'n'Bits is very useful.

Its location on the CD is:

\APPS\CONVERT\IMA\

Paint Shop Pro 3

Paint Shop Pro 3 is a powerful graphics viewing and editing utility that supports about 20 different graphics file formats, including the common GIF and JPEG formats found on the Web. Paint Shop Pro 3 has a host of features for editing and manipulating graphics, and rivals commercial packages with its number and variety of filters and special effects. Paint Shop Pro 3 includes a screen-capture program.

Its location on the CD is:

\APPS\CONVERT\PAINTSHP\

WinJPEG

WinJPEG is a Windows-based graphics-file viewer and converter. You can read and save TIFF, GIF, JPG, TGA, BMP, and PCX file formats with WinJPEG and it has several color-enhancement and dithering features. WinJPEG supports batch conversions and screen captures.

Its location on the CD is:

\APPS\CONVERT\WINJPG\

WinLab

WinLab is a powerful graphics viewer and editor. In addition to WinLabs image processing features, it has built-in TWAIN and network support and a Winsock-compliant application for sending and receiving images.

Its location on the CD is:

\APPS\CONVERT\WINLAB\

Index

Symbols

—> comment (HTML), 174

symbol (HTML), 118

/ (forward slash) (HTML), 45

<!— comment (HTML), 174

A

</A> closing anchor (linking) tag (HMTL), 109

<A> anchor (linking) tag (HTML), 109, 115-119

ABSMIDDLE alignment option, graphics, 98

accessories (World Wide Web)

    Launcher, 231

    URL Grabber Demo, 231

<ADDRESS> tags (HTML), 44-46

addresses, URL, 213-216

  Arena browser, 32

  audio clips, 131

  Audio File Format FAQs, 130

Brang, 126-127

Coca-Cola home page, 27

COMPUNET SERVICES, INC., 210

counters, 145-147

ESPN SportsZone home page, 27

famous people/ speeches, 131

Forsmark college (Germany) counter, 145-146

FTP (Hotdog), 149

Geocities—Beverly Hills Pages, 205

Guest Book, 166

HAL Validation Service, 180

Hotdog home page, 33

HTML 3.0 information, 202

HTML standards, 179

HTMLChek (HTML), 183

Interactive Chat, 166

Java home page, 203

Loginet Incorporated, 209

Lycos, 194

Lynx browser, 32

Mirksy's Worst of the Web, 188

Mosaic browser, 32

movie audio clips, 130

movie/TV clips, 135

My Personal Page home page, 25

NCSA What's New Home Page, 189-190

Netscape extensions home page, 179

Netscape What's New Page, 190

NJ Computer Connection (NJCC), 208

Official World Wide Web Yellow Pages, 193

Politically Correct Bedtime Stories book address, 126

Prodigy, 210

ProTech Specialists Inc., 206

Ripco, 208

Roxanne's home page, 25

Star Wars film script, 125

Start Trek Voyager, 127-128

I-J-K

S

T

GET CONNECTED
to the ultimate source of computer information!

The MCP Forum on CompuServe

Go online with the world's leading computer book publisher!
Macmillan Computer Publishing offers everything
you need for computer success!

Find the books that are right for you!
A complete online catalog, plus sample
chapters and tables of contents give
you an in-depth look at all our books.
The best way to shop or browse!

➤ Get fast answers and technical support for
MCP books and software

➤ Join discussion groups on major computer
subjects

➤ Interact with our expert authors via e-mail
and conferences

➤ Download software from our immense
library:

  ▷ Source code from books
  ▷ Demos of hot software
  ▷ The best shareware and freeware
  ▷ Graphics files

Join now and get a free CompuServe Starter Kit!

To receive your free CompuServe Introductory Membership, call **1-800-848-
8199** and ask for representative #597.

The Starter Kit includes:
➤ Personal ID number and password
➤ $15 credit on the system
➤ Subscription to *CompuServe Magazine*

Once on the CompuServe System, type:

GO MACMILLAN

for the most computer information anywhere!

MACMILLAN
COMPUTER
PUBLISHING

CompuServe

SoftQuad

HoTMetaL PRO™

Create and publish Web pages faster and more easily with the first commercial quality HTML word processor for Windows, Mac and Unix.

Powerful Word Processing Features

- Spell-checker, thesaurus, and dictionary
- Built-in graphical table editor and table support
- Home Page and other useful templates
- Forms support
- In-line graphics display

Easy-to-use Markup Tools

- Insert Element: Choose from a list of only-valid elements
- Edit Links & Attributes: Add hypertext links easily
- Rules Checking & Validation: Ensure correct HTML markup
- TIDY: Import any HTML document, including an invalid document

"A serious product for creating high quality HTML pages ... With HoTMetaL, it's almost certain you'll get your HTML document correct on the first try."
PC Computing

"... leading-edge technology."
PC Magazine

"The current Windows HTML editor of choice."
Boardwatch Magazine

"SoftQuad...has created a set of software applications that connect today's pre-press world to the virtual press of tomorrow's Web page publishing."
Graphic Exchange Magazine

SoftQuad Panorama PRO

View the Wider World of SGML on the World Wide Web

Introducing SoftQuad Panorama PRO, the first SGML browser for the World Wide Web. By putting SGML on the Web, SoftQuad Panorama PRO gives users and publishers access to longer and more complex documents than are currently available, finer control of their display, more powerful searching, broader presentation and style features, and enhanced linking capabilities.

Order your copy of HoTMetaL PRO ($195 US) or Panorama PRO ($139 US) today. Complete this form, then return it by fax or mail. Or, place your order directly from SoftQuad's Web site or by email.

Please place my order for:

☐ HoTMetaL PRO ☐ Panorama PRO

Platform: _____
Operating System:_____
Name: _____
Title:_____
Company: _____
Address: _____
_____
Phone#: _____
Fax#: _____
PO# or Credit Card#:_____

Complete and Return this Card
for a *FREE* Computer Book Catalog

Thank you for purchasing this book! You have purchased a superior computer book written expressly for your needs. To continue to provide the kind of up-to-date, pertinent coverage you've come to expect from us, we need to hear from you. Please take a minute to complete and return this self-addressed, postage-paid form. In return, we'll send you a free catalog of all our computer books on topics ranging from word processing to programming and the internet.

Mr. ☐　　Mrs. ☐　　Ms. ☐　　Dr. ☐

Name (first) [ ] (M.I.) [ ] (last) [ ]

Address [ ]

[ ]

City [ ] State [ ] Zip [ ] [ ]

Phone [ ] Fax [ ] [ ]

Company Name [ ]

E-mail address [ ]

1. Please check at least (3) influencing factors for purchasing this book.

Front or back cover information on book .... ☐
Special approach to the content .... ☐
Completeness of content .... ☐
Author's reputation .... ☐
Publisher's reputation .... ☐
Book cover design or layout .... ☐
Index or table of contents of book .... ☐
Price of book .... ☐
Special effects, graphics, illustrations .... ☐
Other (Please specify): _____ ☐

2. How did you first learn about this book?

Saw in Macmillan Computer Publishing catalog .... ☐
Recommended by store personnel .... ☐
Saw the book on bookshelf at store .... ☐
Recommended by a friend .... ☐
Received advertisement in the mail .... ☐
Saw an advertisement in: _____ ☐
Read book review in: _____ ☐
Other (Please specify): _____ ☐

3. How many computer books have you purchased in the last six months?

This book only .... ☐　　3 to 5 books .... ☐
books .... ☐　　More than 5 .... ☐

4. Where did you purchase this book?

Bookstore .... ☐
Computer Store .... ☐
Consumer Electronics Store .... ☐
Department Store .... ☐
Office Club .... ☐
Warehouse Club .... ☐
Mail Order .... ☐
Direct from Publisher .... ☐
Internet site .... ☐
Other (Please specify): _____ ☐

5. How long have you been using a computer?

☐ Less than 6 months　　☐ 6 months to a year
☐ 1 to 3 years　　☐ More than 3 years

6. What is your level of experience with personal computers and with the subject of this book?

	With PCs	With subject of book
New	☐	☐
Casual	☐	☐
Accomplished	☐	☐
Expert	☐	☐

Source Code ISBN: 0-7897-0621-0

7. Which of the following best describes your job title?

Administrative Assistant .... ☐
Coordinator .... ☐
Manager/Supervisor .... ☐
Director .... ☐
Vice President .... ☐
President/CEO/COO .... ☐
Lawyer/Doctor/Medical Professional .... ☐
Teacher/Educator/Trainer .... ☐
Engineer/Technician .... ☐
Consultant .... ☐
Not employed/Student/Retired .... ☐
Other (Please specify): _____ ☐

8. Which of the following best describes the area of the company your job title falls under?

Accounting .... ☐
Engineering .... ☐
Manufacturing .... ☐
Operations .... ☐
Marketing .... ☐
Sales .... ☐
Other (Please specify): _____ ☐

9. What is your age?

Under 20 .... ☐
21-29 .... ☐
30-39 .... ☐
40-49 .... ☐
50-59 .... ☐
60-over .... ☐

10. Are you:

Male .... ☐
Female .... ☐

11. Which computer publications do you read regularly? (Please list)

_____
_____
_____
_____
_____
_____
_____
_____
_____
_____

Comments: _____
_____
_____

Fold here and scotch-tape to mail.

EXHIBIT B

SOFTWARE LICENSE for QuickTime

PLEASE READ THIS LICENSE CAREFULLY BEFORE USING THE SOFTWARE. BY USING THE SOFTWARE, YOU ARE AGREEING TO BE BOUND BY THE TERMS OF THIS LICENSE. IF YOU DO NOT AGREE TO THE TERMS OF THIS LICENSE, PROMPTLY RETURN THE UNUSED SOFTWARE TO THE PLACE WHERE YOU OBTAINED IT AND YOUR MONEY WILL BE REFUNDED.

1. **License.** The application, demonstration, system and other software accompanying this License, whether on disk, in read-only memory, or on any other media (the "Software"), the related documentation and fonts are licensed to you by Macmillan Computer Publishing. You own the disk on which the Software and fonts are recorded but Macmillan Computer Publishing and/or Macmillan Computer Publishing's Licensors retain title to the Software, related documentation, and fonts. This License allows you to use the Software and fonts on a single Apple computer and make one copy of the Software and fonts in machine-readable form for backup purposes only. You must reproduce on such copy the Macmillan Computer Publishing copyright notice and any other proprietary legends that were on the original copy of the Software and fonts. You may also transfer all your license rights in the Software and fonts, the backup copy of the Software and fonts, the related documentation, and a copy of this License to another party, provided the other party reads and agrees to accept the terms and conditions of this License.

2. **Restrictions.** The Software contains copyrighted material, trade secrets, and other proprietary material. In order to protect them, and except as permitted by applicable legislation, you may not decompile, reverse engineer, disassemble, or otherwise reduce the Software to a human-perceivable form. You may not modify, network, rent, lease, loan, distribute, or create derivative works based upon the Software, in whole or in part. You may not electronically transmit the Software from one computer to another or over a network.

3. **Termination.** This License is effective until terminated. You may terminate this License at any time by destroying the Software, related documentation and fonts, and all copies thereof. This License will terminate immediately without notice from Macmillan Computer Publishing if you fail to comply with any provision of this License. Upon termination you must destroy the Software, related documentation and fonts, and all copies thereof.

4. **Export Law Assurances.** You agree and certify that neither the Software nor any other technical data received from Macmillan Computer Publishing, nor the direct product thereof, will be exported outside the United States except as authorized and as permitted by the laws and regulations of the United States. If the Software has been rightfully obtained by you outside of the United States, you agree that you will not re-export the Software nor any other technical data received from Macmillan Computer Publishing, nor the direct product thereof, except as permitted by the laws and regulations of the United States and the laws and regulations of the jurisdiction in which you obtained the Software.

5. **Government End Users.** If you are acquiring the Software and fonts on behalf of any unit or agency of the United States Government, the following provisions apply. The Government agrees:

    (i) if the Software and fonts are supplied to the Department of Defense (DoD), the Software and fonts are classified as "Commercial Computer Software" and the Government is acquiring only "restricted rights" in the Software, its documentation and fonts as that term is defined in Clause 252.227-7013(c)(1) or the DFARS; and

    (ii) if the Software and fonts are supplied to any unit or agency of the United States Government other than DoD, the Government's rights in the Software, its documentation and fonts will be as defined in Clause 52.227-19(c)(2) of the FAR or, in the case of NASA, in Clause 18-52.227-86(d) of the NASA supplement to the FAR.

6. **Limited Warranty on Media.** Macmillan Computer Publishing warrants the diskettes and/or compact disc on which the Software and fonts are recorded to be free from defects in materials and workmanship under normal use for a period of ninety (90) days from the date of purchase as evidenced by a copy of the receipt. Macmillan Computer Publishing's entire liability and your exclusive remedy will be replacement of the diskettes and/or compact disc not meeting Macmillan Computer Publishing's limited warranty and which is returned to Macmillan Computer Publishing or a Macmillan Computer Publishing authorized representative with a copy of the receipt. Macmillan Computer Publishing will have no responsibility to replace a disk/disc

damaged by accident, abuse, or misapplication. ANY IMPLIED WAR-
RANTIES ON THE DISKETTES AND/OR COMPACT DISC, INCLUDING
THE IMPLIED WARRANTIES OF MERCHANTABILITY AND FITNESS
FOR A PARTICULAR PURPOSE, ARE LIMITED IN DURATION TO
NINETY (90) DAYS FROM THE DATE OF DELIVERY. THIS WARRANTY
GIVES YOU SPECIFIC LEGAL RIGHTS, AND YOU MAY ALSO HAVE
OTHER RIGHTS WHICH VARY BY JURISDICTION.

7. **Disclaimer of Warranty on Apple Software.** You expressly ac-
knowledge and agree that use of the Software and fonts is at your sole
risk. The Software, related documentation, and fonts are provided "AS
IS" and without warranty of any kind and Macmillan Computer Pub-
lishing and Macmillan Computer Publishing's Licensor(s) (for the pur-
poses of provisions 7 and 8, Macmillan Computer Publishing and
Macmillan Computer Publishing's Licensor(s) shall be collectively re-
ferred to as "Macmillan Computer Publishing") EXPRESSLY DISCLAIM
ALL WARRANTIES, EXPRESS OR IMPLIED, INCLUDING, BUT NOT
LIMITED TO, THE IMPLIED WARRANTIES OF MERCHANTABILITY
AND FITNESS FOR A PARTICULAR PURPOSE. MACMILLAN COM-
PUTER PUBLISHING DOES NOT WARRANT THAT THE FUNCTIONS
CONTAINED IN THE SOFTWARE WILL MEET YOUR REQUIREMENTS,
OR THAT THE OPERATION OF THE SOFTWARE WILL BE UNINTER-
RUPTED OR ERROR-FREE, OR THAT DEFECTS IN THE SOFTWARE AND
THE FONTS WILL BE CORRECTED. FURTHERMORE, MACMILLAN
COMPUTER PUBLISHING DOES NOT WARRANT OR MAKE ANY REP-
RESENTATIONS REGARDING THE USE OR THE RESULTS OF THE USE
OF THE SOFTWARE AND FONTS OR RELATED DOCUMENTATION IN
TERMS OF THEIR CORRECTNESS, ACCURACY, RELIABILITY, OR OTH-
ERWISE. NO ORAL OR WRITTEN INFORMATION OR ADVICE GIVEN
BY MACMILLAN COMPUTER PUBLISHING OR A MACMILLAN COM-
PUTER PUBLISHING AUTHORIZED REPRESENTATIVE SHALL CREATE
A WARRANTY OR IN ANY WAY INCREASE THE SCOPE OF THIS WAR-
RANTY. SHOULD THE SOFTWARE PROVE DEFECTIVE, YOU (AND
NOT MACMILLAN COMPUTER PUBLISHING OR A MACMILLAN
COMPUTER PUBLISHING AUTHORIZED REPRESENTATIVE) ASSUME
THE ENTIRE COST OF ALL NECESSARY SERVICING, REPAIR OR COR-
RECTION. SOME JURISDICTIONS DO NOT ALLOW THE EXCLUSION
OF IMPLIED WARRANTIES, SO THE ABOVE EXCLUSION MAY NOT
APPLY TO YOU.

8. **Limitation of Liability.** UNDER NO CIRCUMSTANCES INCLUDING NEGLIGENCE, SHALL MACMILLAN COMPUTER PUBLISHING BE LIABLE FOR ANY INCIDENTAL, SPECIAL, OR CONSEQUENTIAL DAMAGES THAT RESULT FROM THE USE OR INABILITY TO USE THE SOFTWARE OR RELATED DOCUMENTATION, EVEN IF MACMILLAN COMPUTER PUBLISHING OR A MACMILLAN COMPUTER PUBLISH-ING AUTHORIZED REPRESENTATIVE HAS BEEN ADVISED OF THE POSSIBILITY OF SUCH DAMAGES. SOME JURISDICTIONS DO NOT ALLOW THE LIMITATION OR EXCLUSION OF LIABILITY FOR INCIDENTAL OR CONSEQUENTIAL DAMAGES SO THE ABOVE LIMITATION OR EXCLUSION MAY NOT APPLY TO YOU.

    In no event shall Macmillan Computer Publishing's total liability to you for all damages, losses, and causes of action (whether in contract, tort [including negligence] or otherwise) exceed the amount paid by you for the Software and fonts.

9. **Law and Severability.** This License shall be governed by and con-strued in accordance with the laws of the United States and the State of California, as applied to agreements entered into and to be performed entirely within California between California residents. If for any rea-son a court of competent jurisdiction finds any provision of this Li-cense, or portion thereof, to be unenforceable, that provision of the License shall be enforced to the maximum extent permissible so as to effect the intent of the parties, and the remainder of this License shall continue in full force and effect.

10. **Complete Agreement.** This License constitutes the entire agreement between the parties with respect to the use of the Software, the related documentation and fonts, and supersedes all prior or contemporaneous understandings or agreements, written or oral, regarding such subject matter. No amendment to or modification of this License will be bind-ing unless in writing and signed by a duly authorized representative of Macmillan Computer Publishing.